IF THE RAINDROPS UNITED

Also by Judah Friedlander

How to Beat Up Anybody: An Instructional and Inspirational Karate Book by the World Champion

IF THE RAINDROPS UNITED

Drawings and Cartoons

JUDAH FRIEDLANDER

hachette
BOOKS
New York Boston

Hachette Books
Hachette Book Group
1290 Avenue of the Americas
New York, NY 10104

HachetteBookGroup.com

Printed in the United States of America

RRD-C

First Edition: October 2015

10 9 8 7 6 5 4 3 2 1

Hachette Books is a division of Hachette Book Group, Inc.

The Hachette Books name and logo are trademarks of Hachette Book Group, Inc.

The publisher is not responsible for websites (or their content) that are not owned by the publisher.

Library of Congress Control Number 2015947599

ISBN 978-0-316-30695-9 (Hardcover ed.);
ISBN 978-0-316-30696-6 (Ebook ed.)

DEDICATION (definition)

A ploy authors use in an attempt to add gravitas to their book.

Seriously though...

I dedicate this book to my Mom, who always did a lot of art, and passed it on to me. I also dedicate this book to my Dad, who taught me to always question authority.

INTRODUCTION (definition)

A contrivance authors use to secretly add more pages to their book.

Warning: This is a book of drawings. If you're looking for a book with a lot of words, you've made a mistake.

Bonus Warning: Most of these drawings are comedy. But some are serious. Or just weird.

I've been doing stand-up since I was 19. But I've been drawing since I was a kid.

Here's one I did when I was 10.

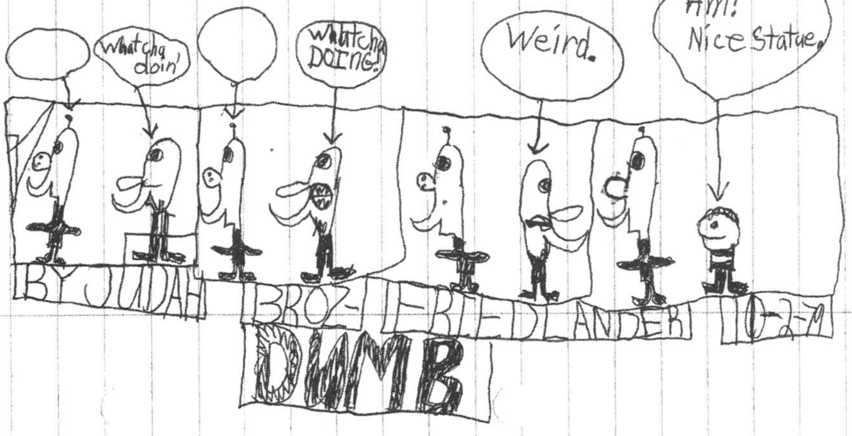

Whatcha doin'
Whatcha DOING!
Weird.
Hm! Nice Statue.
BY JUDAH
BROZ-FRIEDLANDER
10-2-79
DUMB

When I was 11, I did this political cartoon about Polish human rights leader Lech Walesa.

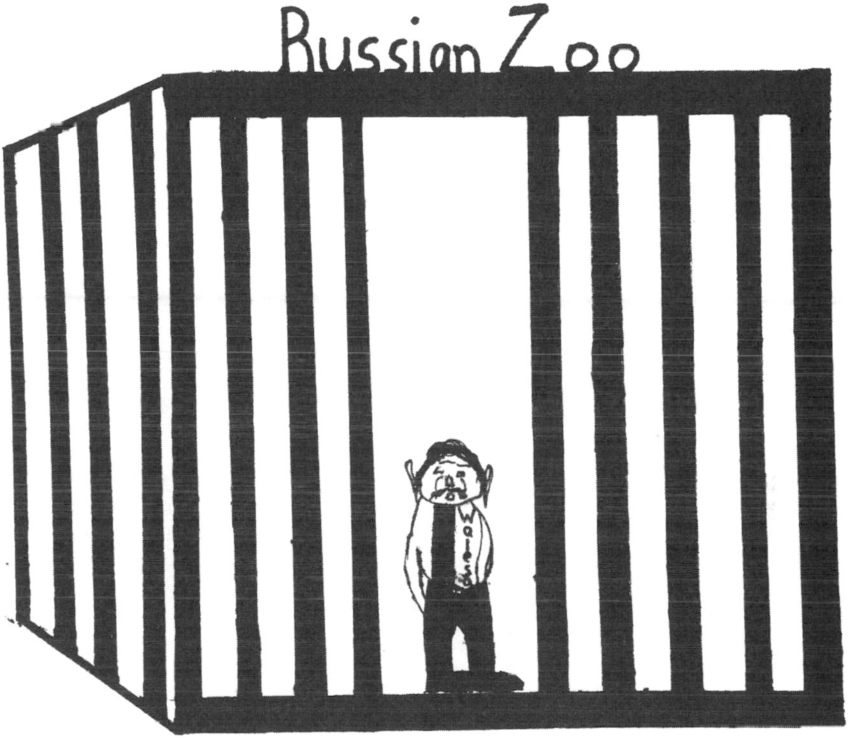
Russian Zoo
Walesa

Introductions are awkward.
So...

Uhh...

That's the end

of the

Introduction.

IF THE RAINDROPS UNITED

RABBIT RUNNING ACROSS THE FIELD WEARING
A HUMAN FOOT FOR GOOD LUCK

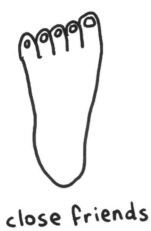

close friends

acquaintances

enemies

lovers

Scalene triangle.

Scalene triangle after corrective surgery at the Isosceles Beautification Institute.

Sometimes, you should just let go.

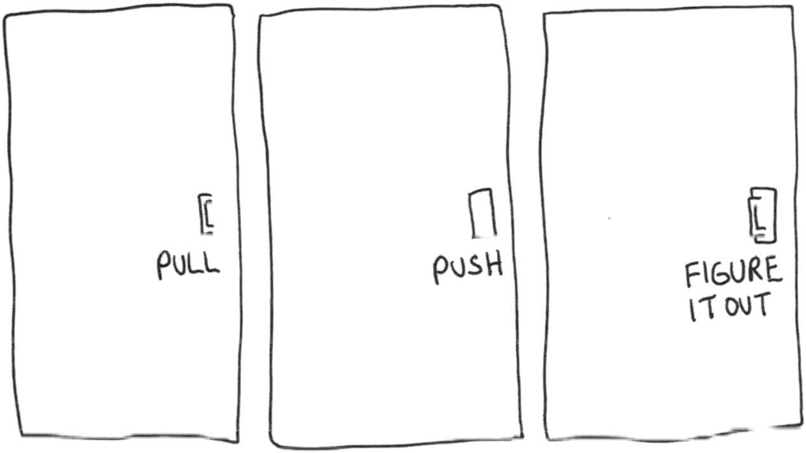
PULL
PUSH
FIGURE IT OUT

PASSIVE-AGGRESSIVE DOOR

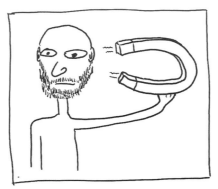

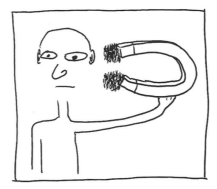

ACORNS FALL OUT OF TREES.
THAT'S WHY THEY WEAR HELMETS.

SUPERHERO'S FLYING SECRET EXPOSED

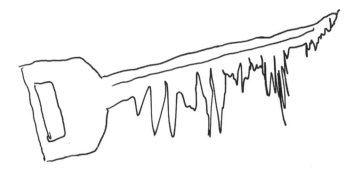

THE KEY TO "HAPPINESS"

SPIDER SHOEBOX

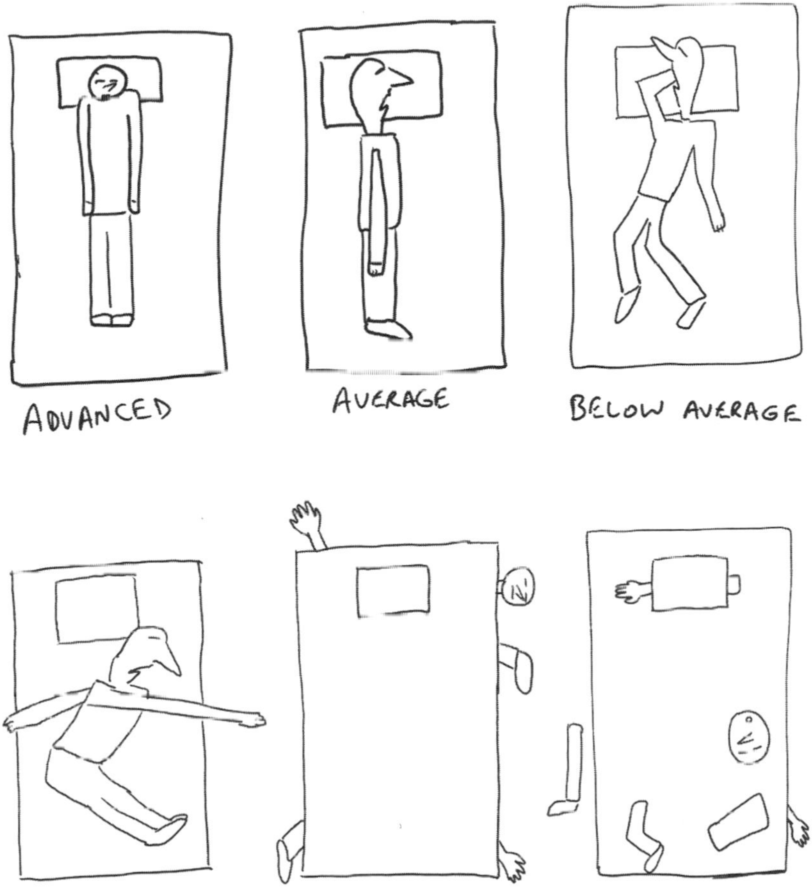
ADVANCED
AVERAGE
BELOW AVERAGE
BAD
WAY OFF
TERRIBLE

The last teepee in Manhattan.
Rent $10,000/month.

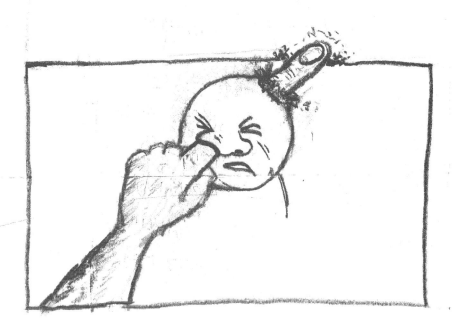

PICK YOUR OWN NOSE. OR SOMEONE WILL DO IT FOR YOU.

Algebra

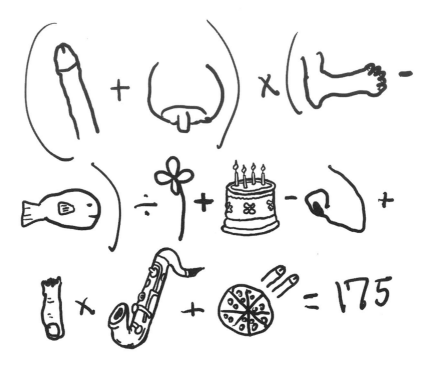

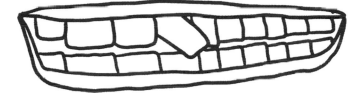

A lone tooth bravely fights
against fascism.

AFTER 6 MONTHS, TODD MASTERED
THE TWO-WHEELED UNICYCLE

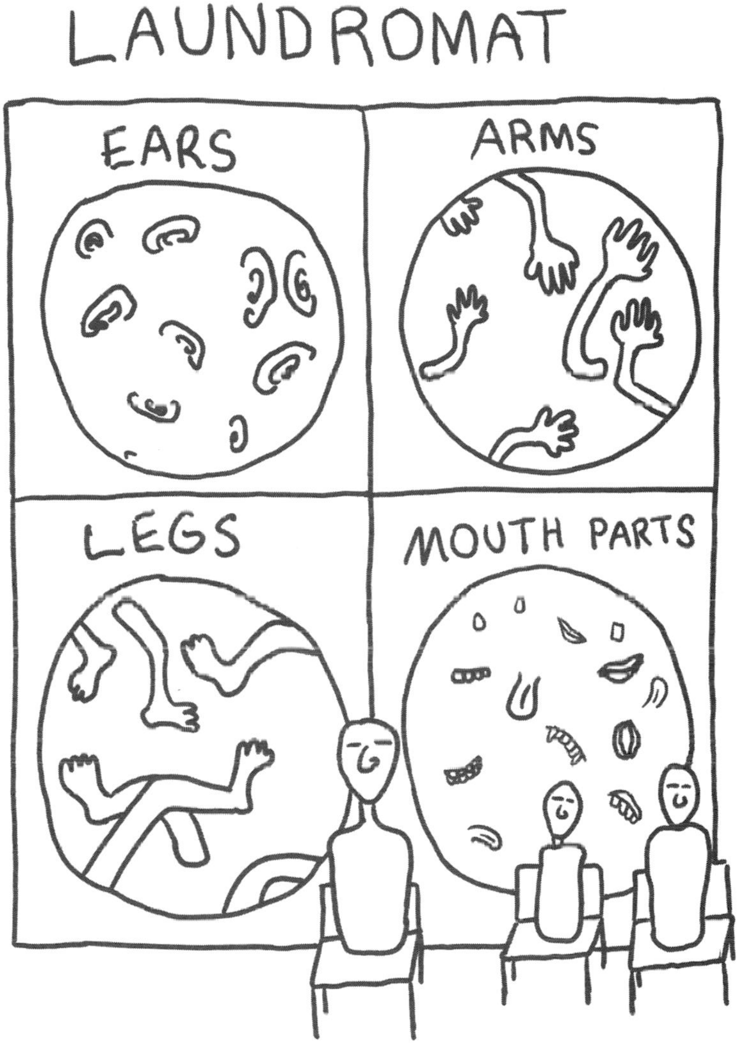
LAUNDROMAT
EARS
ARMS
LEGS
MOUTH PARTS

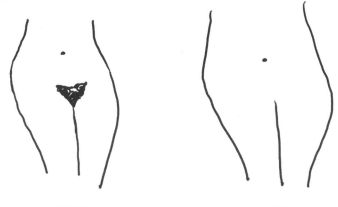

YES   NO

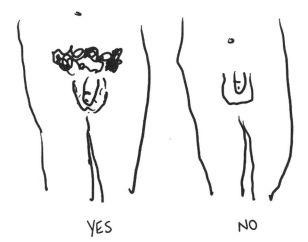

YES   NO

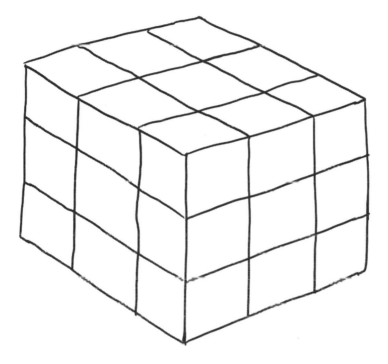

GENTRIFIED RUBIK'S CUBE

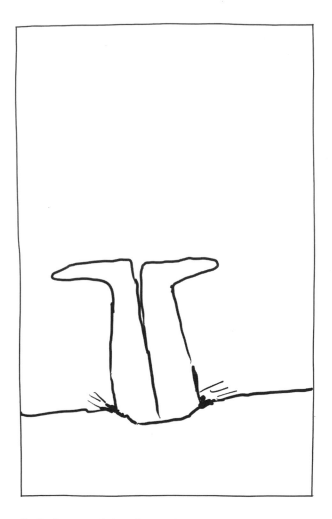

Ballerina crash-landing in first position.

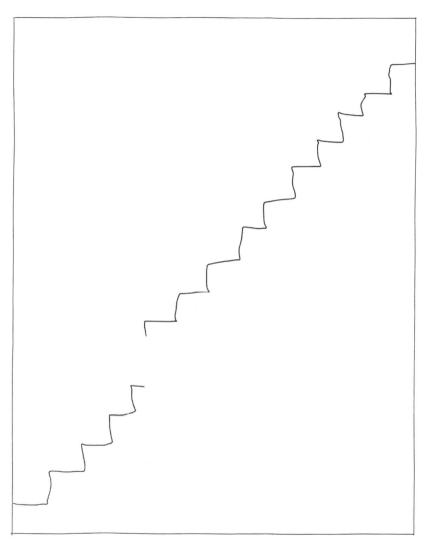

OUT OF STEP

THE AMERICAN WAY

PROVIDING MORE FREE HOUSING
THAN ANY OTHER COUNTRY

HUMAN BRAIN

FEAR
HATE
"I'M COOL"
DENIAL
OF FEAR
& HATE

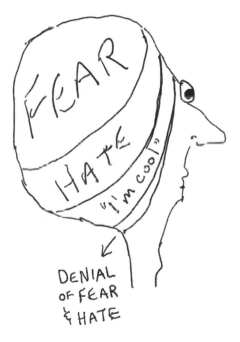

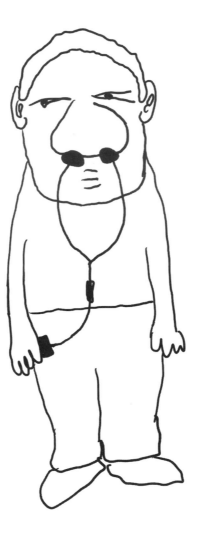

SMELLING THE MUSIC

MANHATTAN COUPLE AT BRUNCH.

THEN ONE NIGHT, THE DISHES DID JEFFREY.

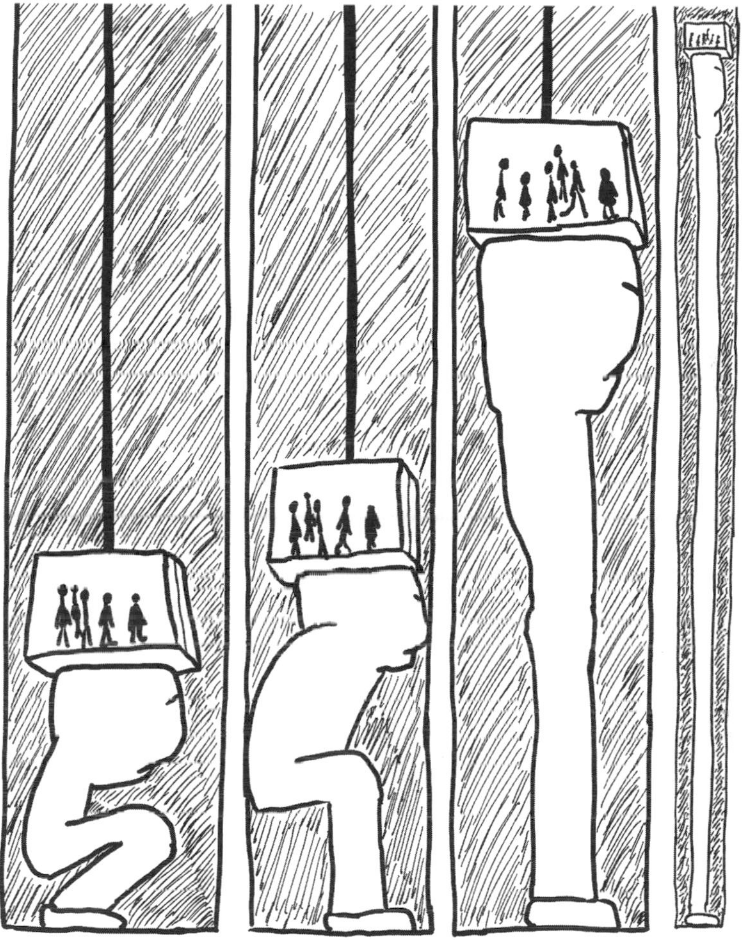

HOW ELEVATORS WORK

2015

WAITING HOURS TO BUY $20 GLUTEN-FREE DONUTS

1931

WAITING HOURS HOPING TO GET FREE BREAD

Reach for the stars.
But make sure you're outdoors first.

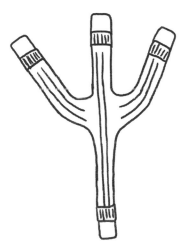

Pencil for person who doesn't have anything to say, but still makes a lot of mistakes.

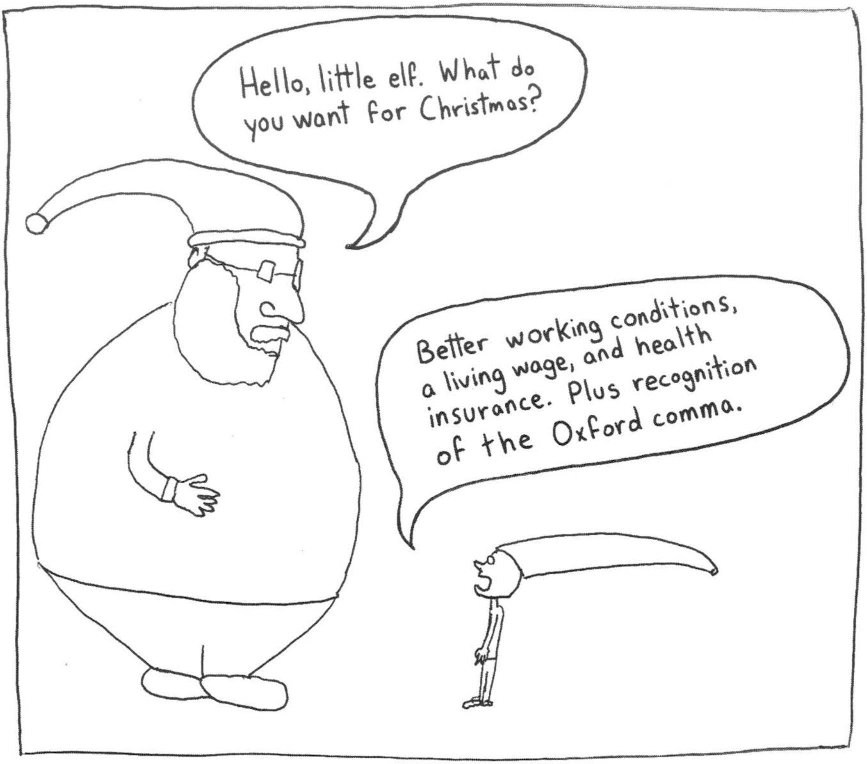
Hello, little elf. What do you want for Christmas?
Better working conditions, a living wage, and health insurance. Plus recognition of the Oxford comma.

KITE'S REVENGE

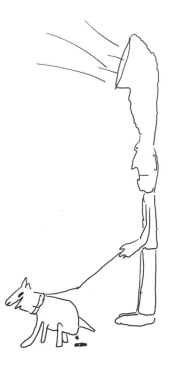

SPARKLES COULD ONLY POOP IF TED PLAYED
SMOOTH JAZZ IN B FLAT.

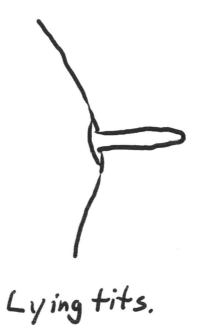

Honest tits. Lying tits.

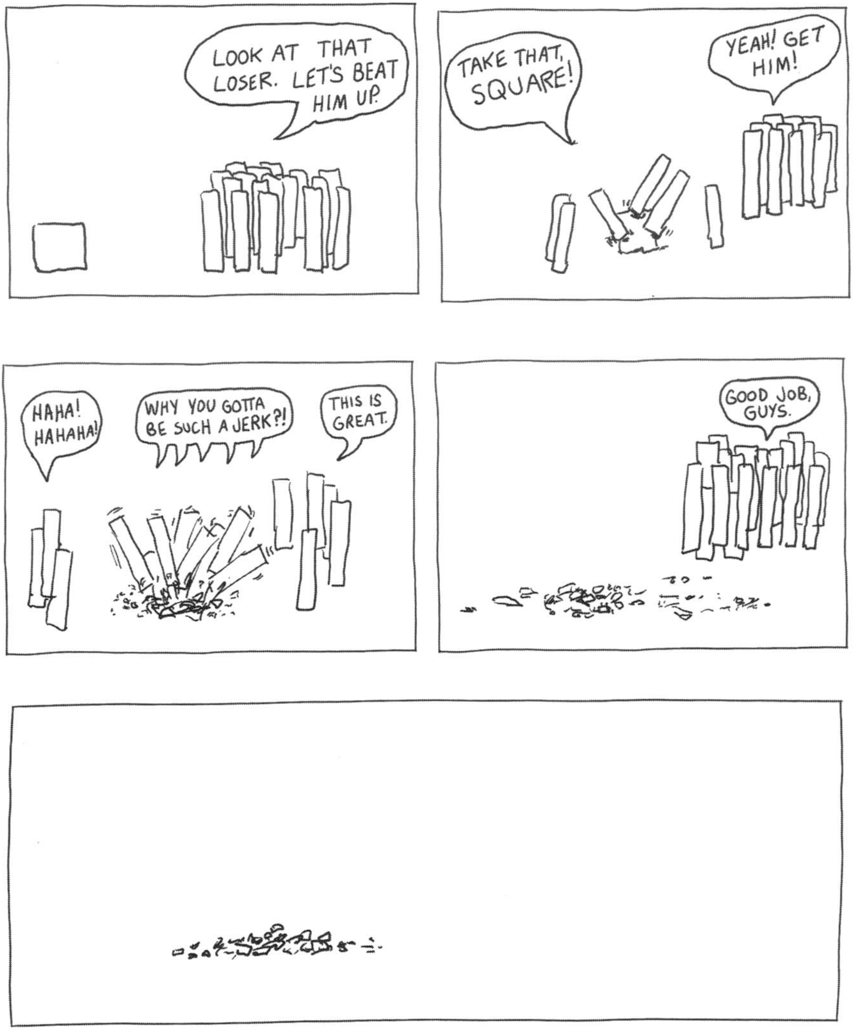
LOOK AT THAT LOSER. LET'S BEAT HIM UP.
TAKE THAT, SQUARE!
YEAH! GET HIM!
HAHA! HAHAHA!
WHY YOU GOTTA BE SUCH A JERK?!
THIS IS GREAT.
GOOD JOB, GUYS.

IN 2054, COCKROACHES
BECAME THE FIRST
TO COLONIZE THE MOON

Funeral of the letter P

Last week the letter P succumbed to pneumonia. A disease it "never even should've been a part of" according to a letter that didn't want to be named. All the letters of the alphabet showed up to mourn. Even the Umlaut and the Enye, who traveled from overseas, attended. The letter P is preceded by the letter O and followed by the letter Q.

MUSHROOM CLOUD PIZZA

On September 15, 2063 humans and cars finally got equal rights.

PARKING METER

STANDING METER

PARKING METER

PARKING METER

In 2044, standing on public sidewalks was banned for humans.

After 19 years of campaigning, humans won the right to stand at former "cars only" parking meters – which came to be known as "standing meters." Standing meters typically cost two dollars every three minutes. Only 17% of meters were designated as standing meters. Despite the high cost and scarcity of standing meters, the zoned legalization of standing was considered a landmark human rights victory. Government studies concluded that standing, in addition to causing pedestrian traffic, also caused the economy to lose income – because people were standing around – instead of shopping. Many conservatives considered standing to be un-American. A small faction of progressives were also against standing rights because they felt that standing was a disrespectful gesture toward paraplegics. An unspoken reason the government was against standing was because it didn't want multiple people standing around – because that could lead to people conversing, thinking, and exchanging ideas. Also of note, by 2040, cars became 100% self-driving.

Pie chart that shows how hungry
I was when I drew this pie chart.

The "Fabulous" '50s

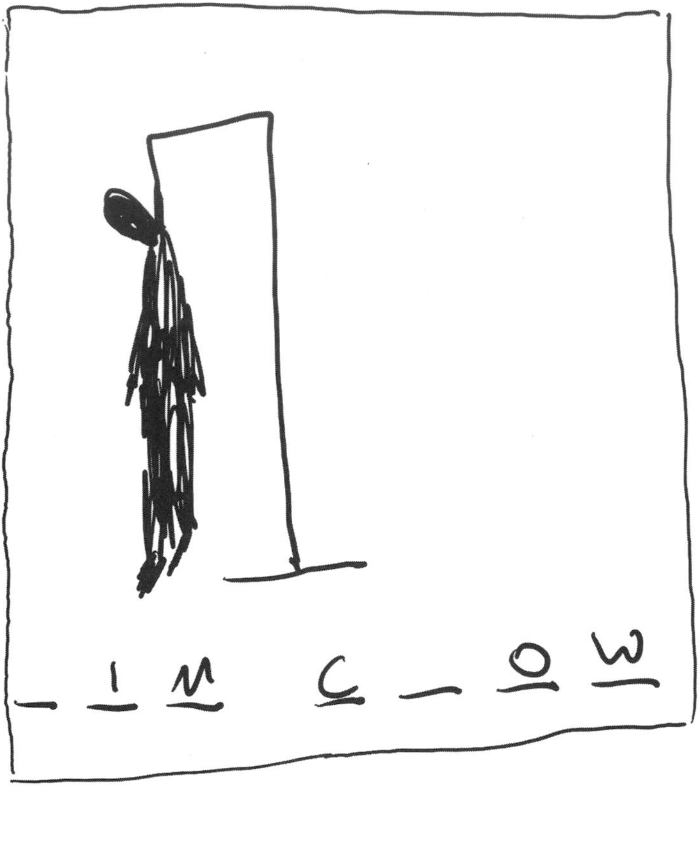
_ I M C _ O W

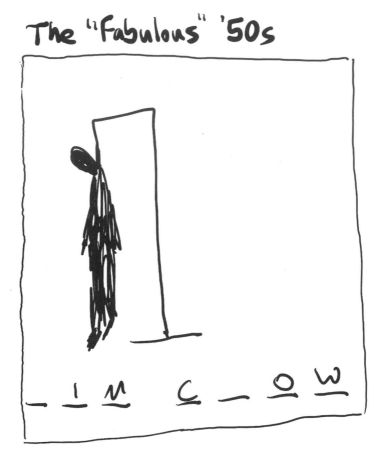

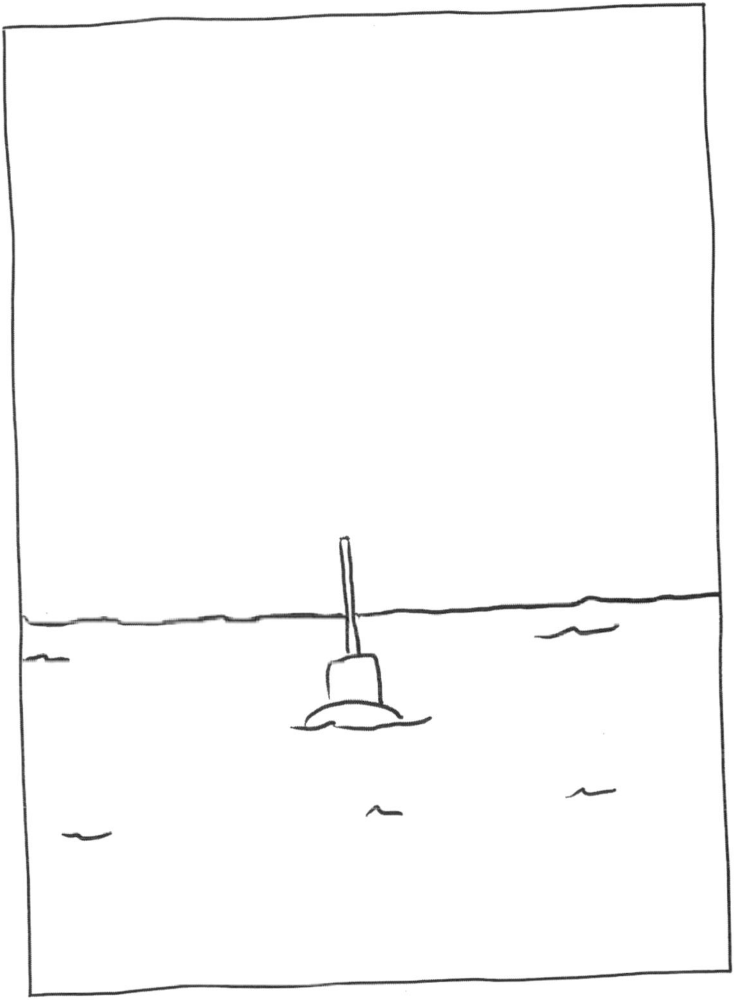

EMPIRE STATE BUILDING YEAR 2178

THE PACIFIED™ BABY CIGARETTE
KEEPS YOUR BABY SATISFIED

MADE IN USA

The Pacified™ baby cigarette is all your baby will ever want.

Never buy another toy because your baby will always be satisfied with the Pacified.™

Keep your baby's weight down while giving it the nicotine it needs!

Say goodbye to crying. The Pacified™ keeps it occupied.

"Helps your baby lose its baby teeth faster, so its adult teeth can come in sooner" say 5 out of 4 dentists.

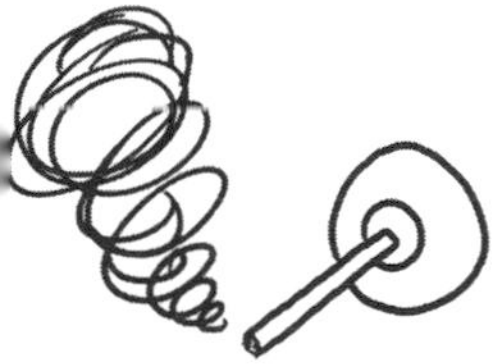

The Pacified™ base is made of 100% asBESTos.™ So your baby will always be safe. The Pacified™ won't burn the baby, and it won't burn the crib you paid so much money for.

The Pacified™ baby cigarette also helps increase constipation. Less pooping means less money you spend on diapers.

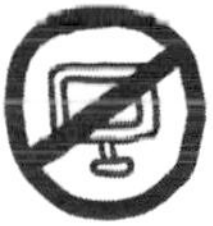

Throw away your baby monitors!
With the Pacified™ you'll always know where your baby is. If you smell smoke, then you know that your baby is nearby, safely smoking.

The Pacified™ baby cigarette.
Keeping parents stress-free since 2054.

PENCIL

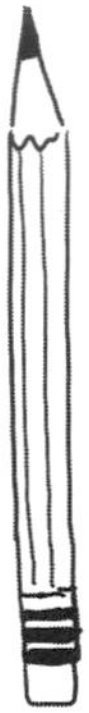

CHILDHOOD

MISTAKES ARE OK BECAUSE YOU HAVE YOUR FRIEND, THE ERASER, WHO WILL MAKE EVERYTHING IN THE WORLD RIGHT AGAIN!

PEN

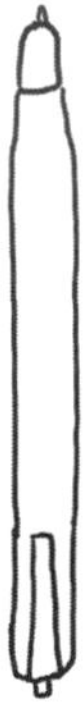

ADULTHOOD

PERMANENT INK. NO ERASER! DON'T FUCK UP!

MECHANICAL PENCIL

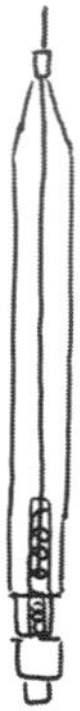

PUBERTY

LOOK AND FEEL LIKE AN ADULT, BUT HAVE THE FREEDOM OF A CHILD.

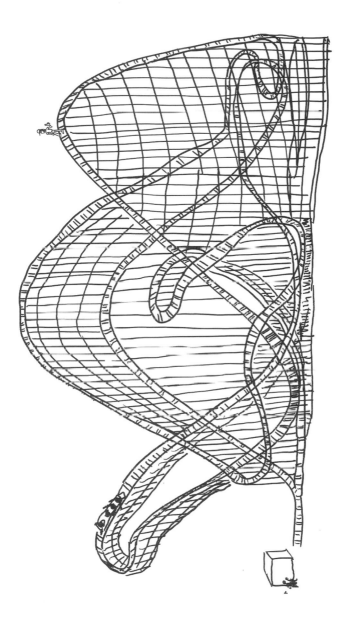

HITCHHIKING

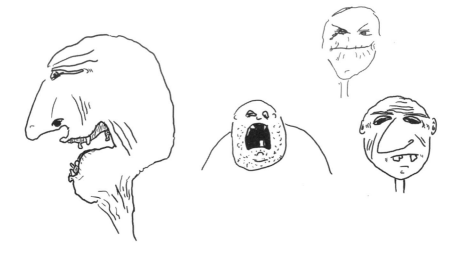

THE CASUAL FLOSSERS

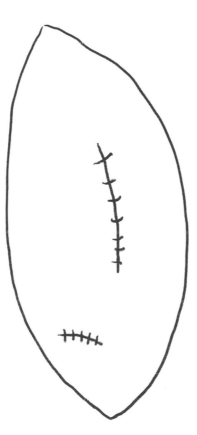

Football who's had its appendix removed.

SCOTT, 16, IS THE OLDEST-LOOKING
IN HIS CLASS.

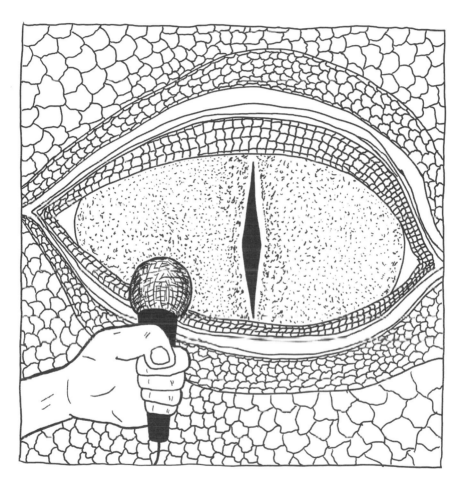

Last night's show had only one audience member, but it was huge.

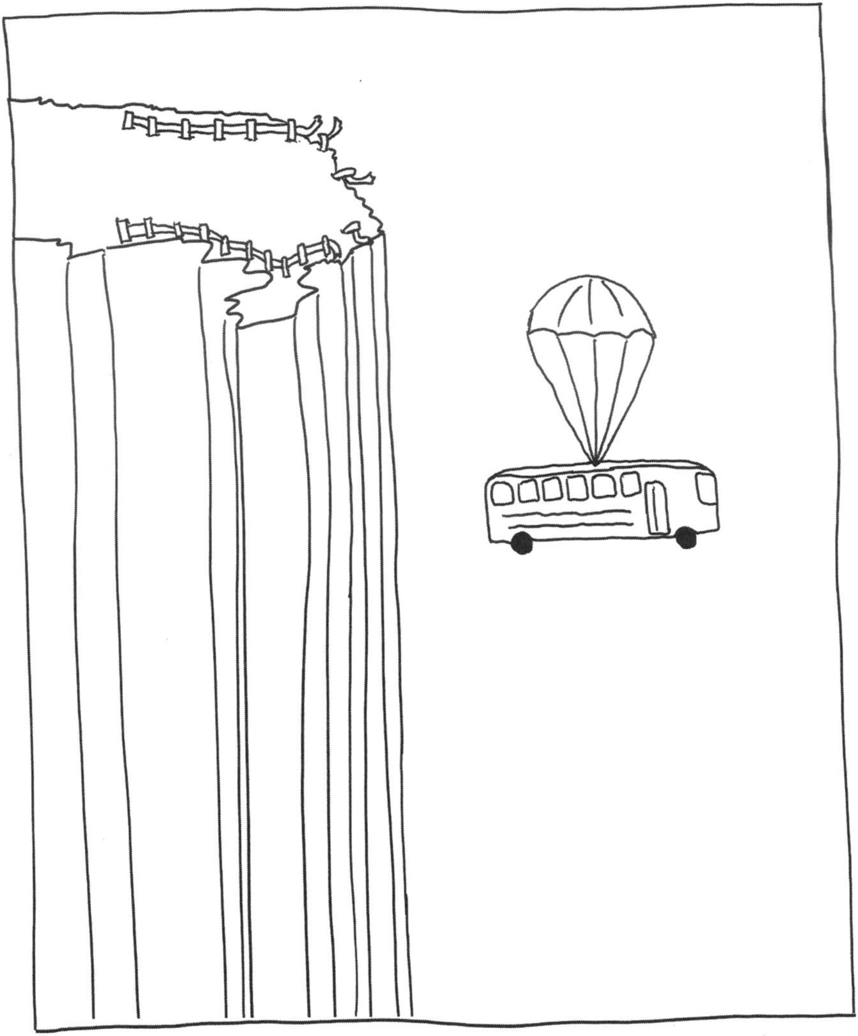

SCHOOL BUS SAFETY IDEA #17

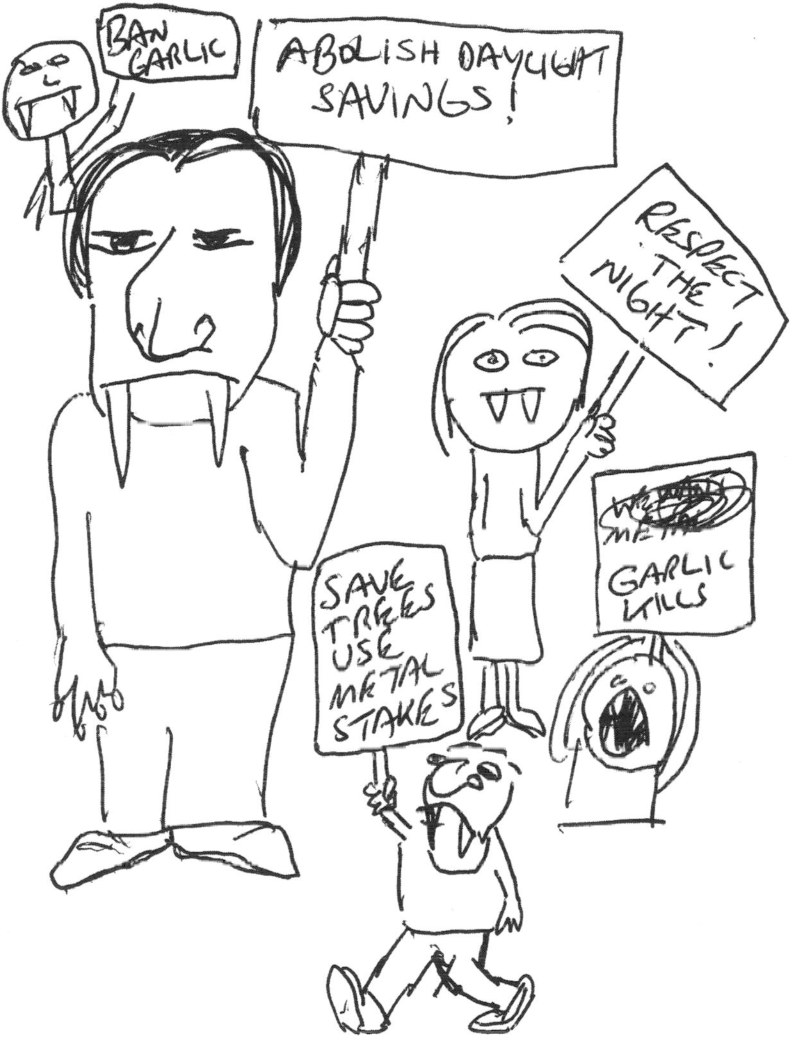
BAN GARLIC
ABOLISH DAYLIGHT SAVINGS!
RESPECT THE NIGHT!
GARLIC KILLS
SAVE TREES USE METAL STAKES

VAMPIRE PROTEST

8th Place Finisher In A
Contest Nobody Entered

FROSTY'S LAST SKI TRIP

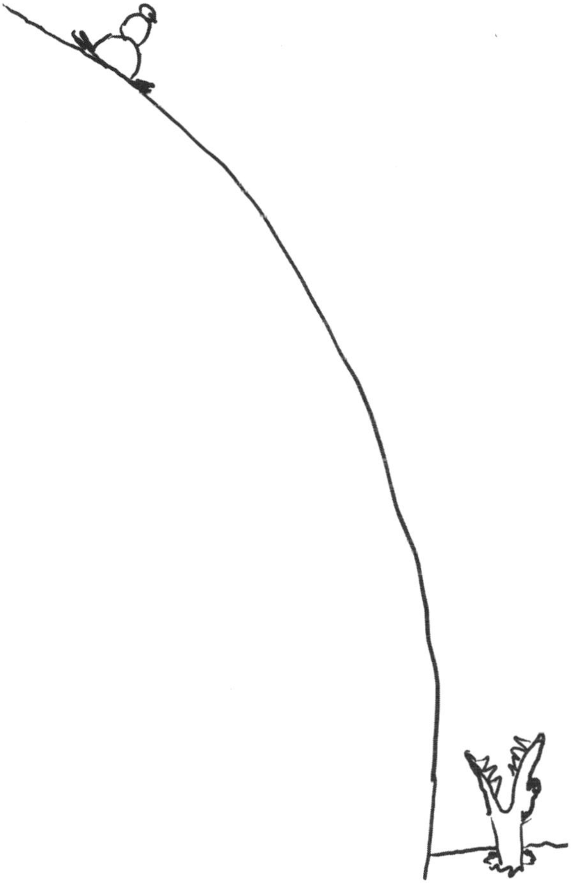

There's a fine line between the shotput and littering.

THE BIG TOE MERGER OF 2085

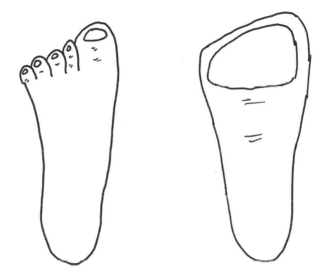

FOOT: PRE 2084   FOOT: POST 2084

THE SMALL TOES GOT BOUGHT OUT
BY THE BIG TOE IN 2085

NOSEMAN

AKA Mr. Fintsworth

Has a smelling power greater than 100 dogs. He can smell corruption from a 1000 miles away. He can shoot his unlimited supply of boogers in any direction and dislocate your kneecaps. He can trap you in a Truth Cocoon of Snot and make you reveal your darkest secrets.

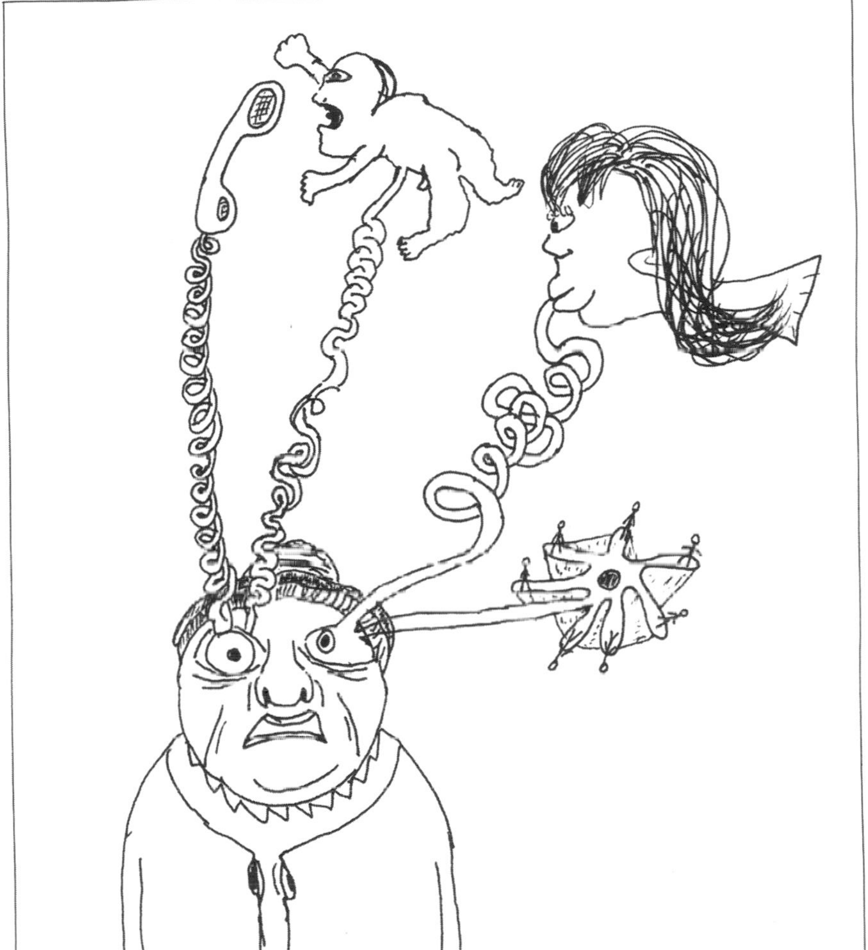

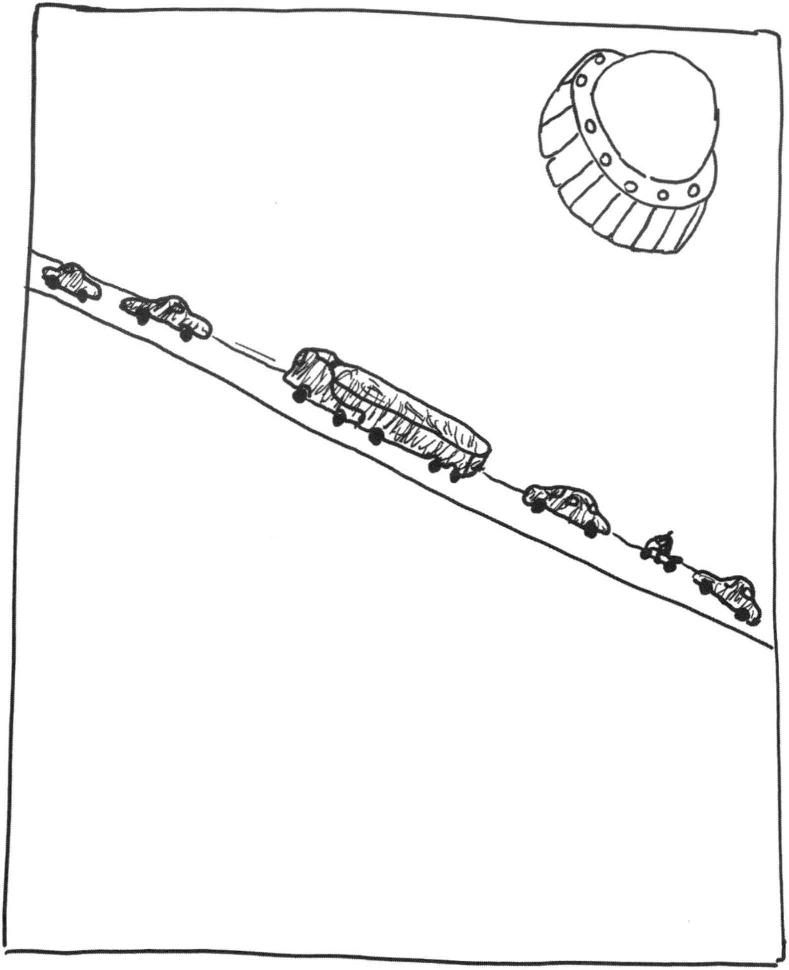

U.F.O. SPOTTED!

WASHING CARS FOR FREE!

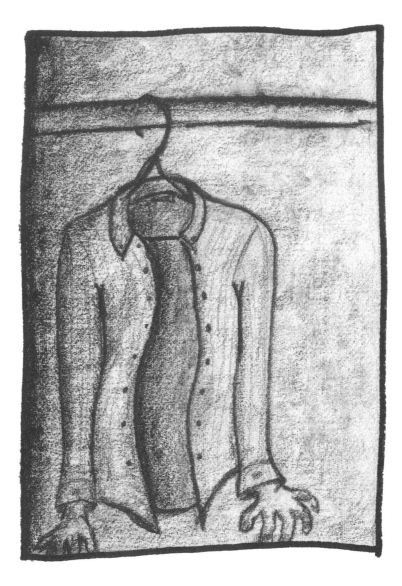

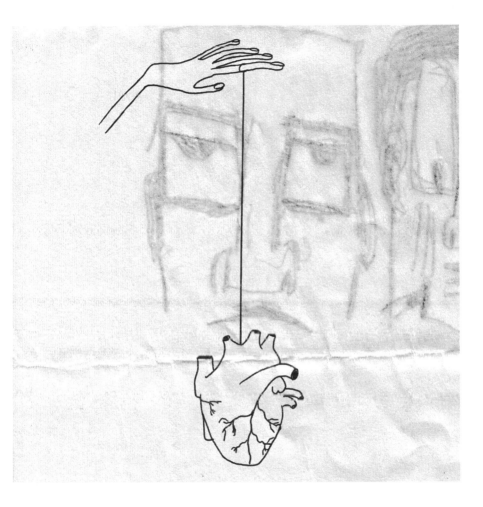

YO-YO HEART

Bigfoot teaches a young rattlesnake how to fly.

DELUXE MULTI-WEAPON WITH MIRROR!

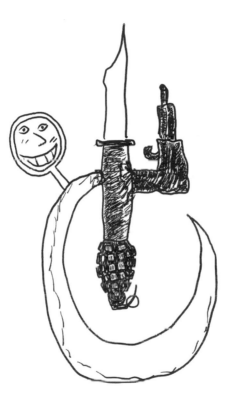

NOW YOU CAN SEE THE GLORY OF
VICTORY IN YOUR EYES WHEN YOU KILL
SOMETHING!

COUSINS

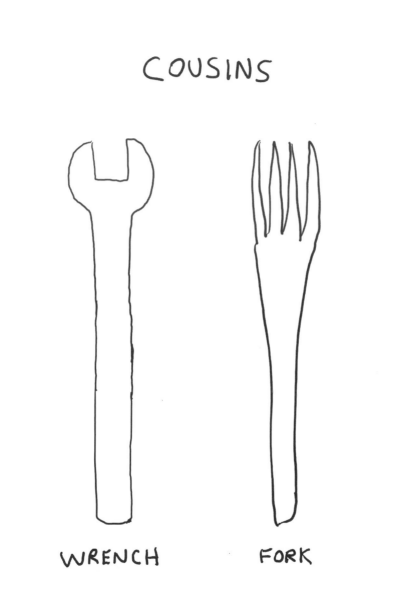

WRENCH   FORK

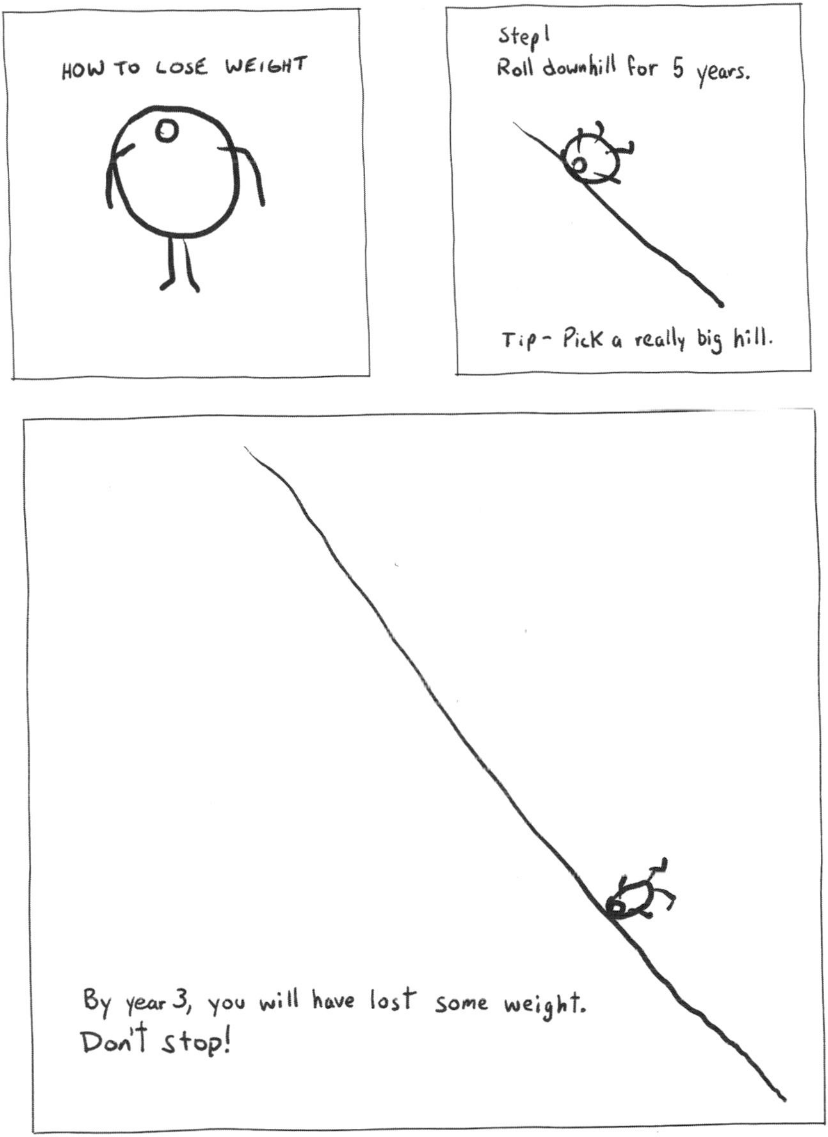
HOW TO LOSE WEIGHT
Step 1
Roll downhill for 5 years.
Tip - Pick a really big hill.
By year 3, you will have lost some weight.
Don't stop!

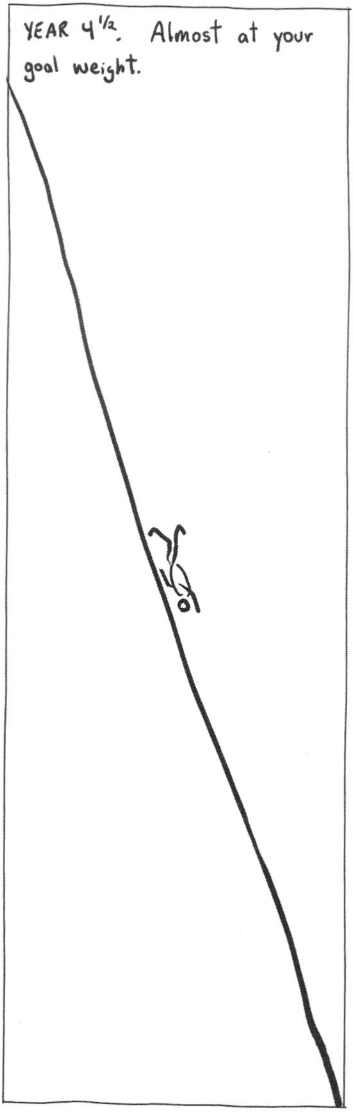
YEAR 4 1/2. Almost at your goal weight.

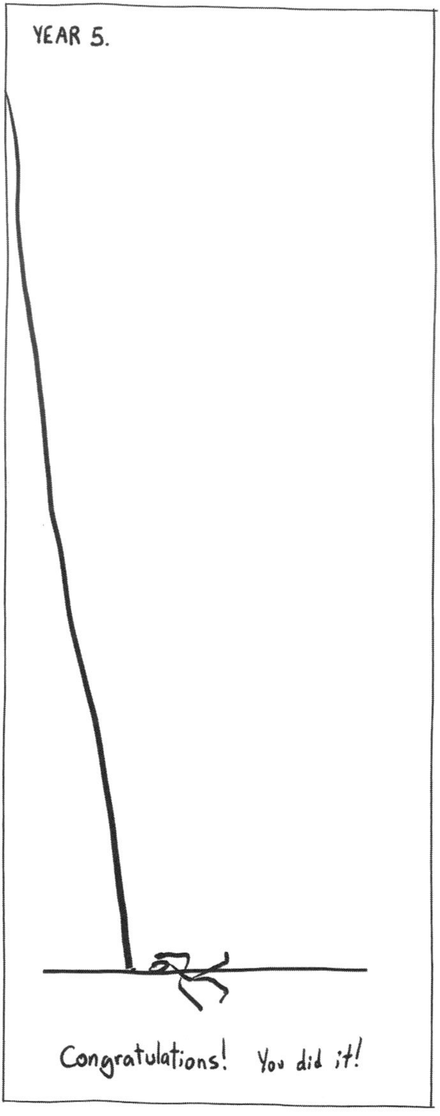
YEAR 5.
Congratulations! You did it!

Remember: Don't get hit by a truck.

Avoid getting eaten by a tarantula.
And remember to stay hydrated.
Congrats again. You look great!

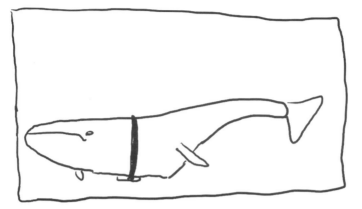

WHALE SUSHI

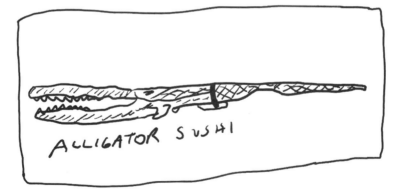

ALLIGATOR SUSHI

FOR PEOPLE WHO LIKE A LARGE
MEAT-TO-RICE RATIO

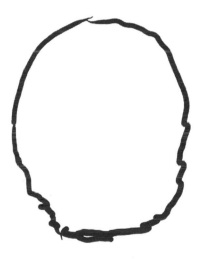

Circle with arthritis.

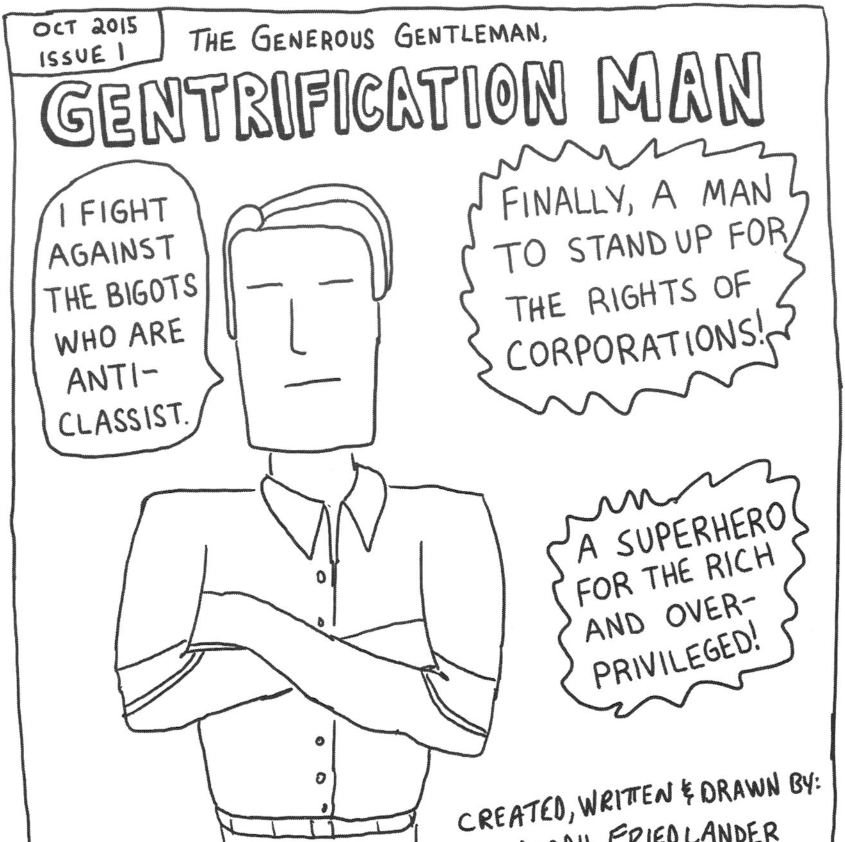
OCT 2015
ISSUE 1
THE GENEROUS GENTLEMAN,
GENTRIFICATION MAN
I FIGHT AGAINST THE BIGOTS WHO ARE ANTI-CLASSIST.
FINALLY, A MAN TO STAND UP FOR THE RIGHTS OF CORPORATIONS!
A SUPERHERO FOR THE RICH AND OVER-PRIVILEGED!
CREATED, WRITTEN & DRAWN BY:
JUDAH FRIEDLANDER

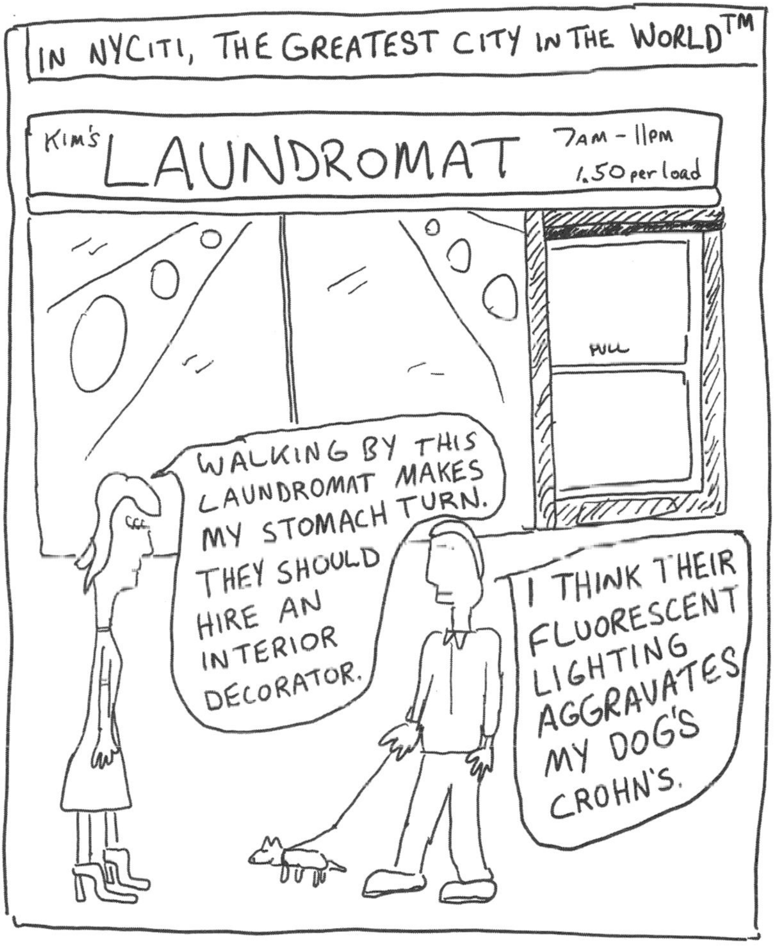
IN NYCITI, THE GREATEST CITY IN THE WORLD™
KIM'S LAUNDROMAT 7AM – 11PM 1.50 per load
PULL
WALKING BY THIS LAUNDROMAT MAKES MY STOMACH TURN. THEY SHOULD HIRE AN INTERIOR DECORATOR.
I THINK THEIR FLUORESCENT LIGHTING AGGRAVATES MY DOG'S CROHN'S.

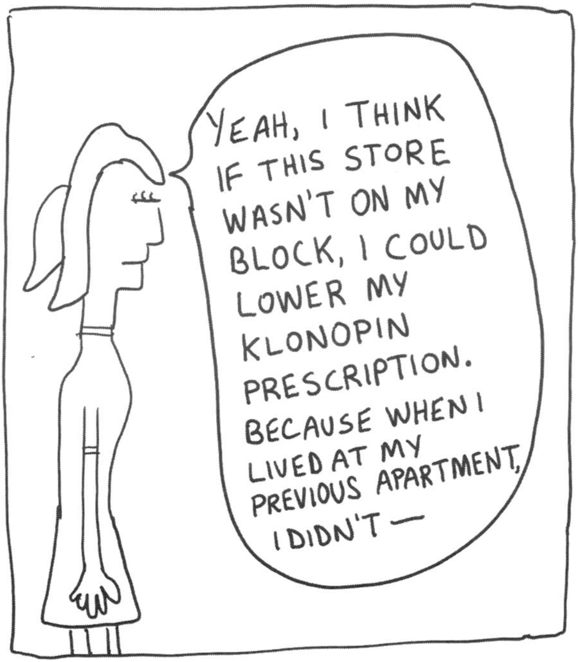
YEAH, I THINK IF THIS STORE WASN'T ON MY BLOCK, I COULD LOWER MY KLONOPIN PRESCRIPTION. BECAUSE WHEN I LIVED AT MY PREVIOUS APARTMENT, I DIDN'T —

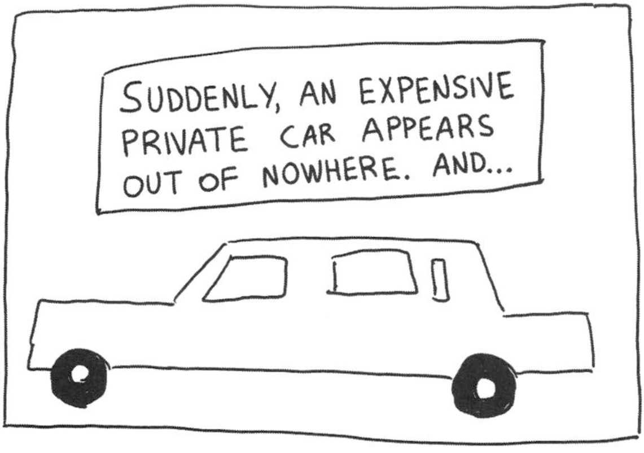
SUDDENLY, AN EXPENSIVE PRIVATE CAR APPEARS OUT OF NOWHERE. AND...

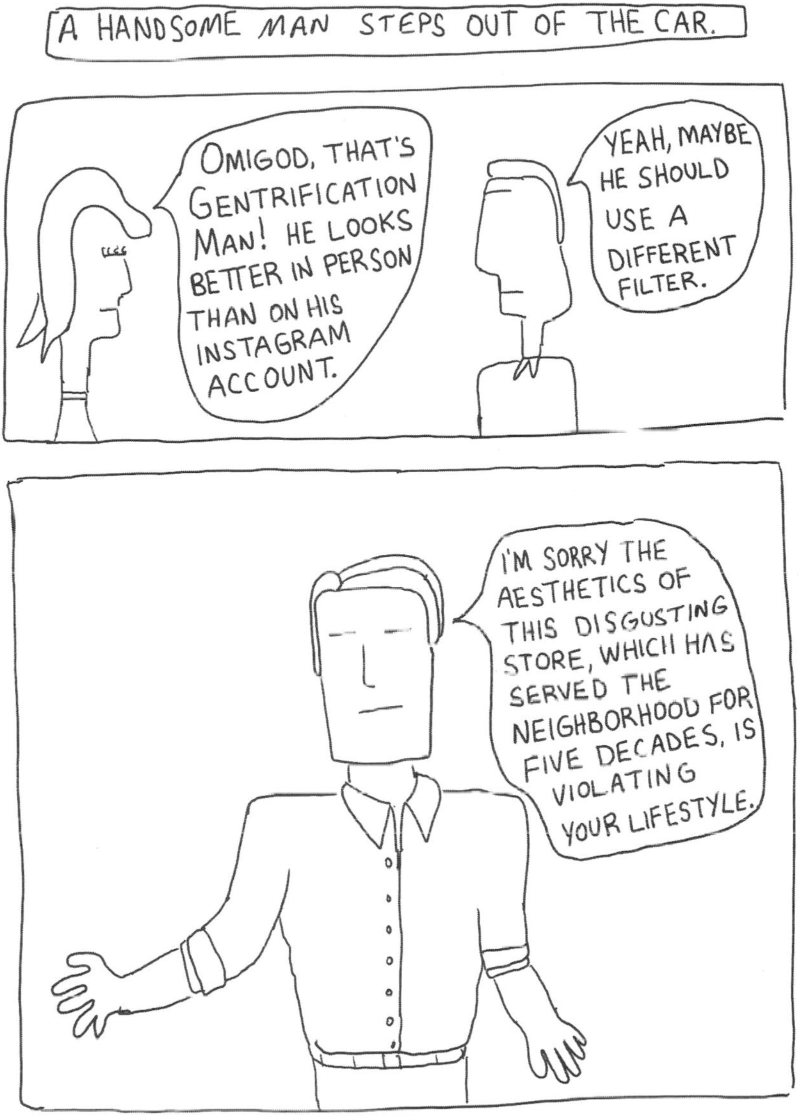
A HANDSOME MAN STEPS OUT OF THE CAR.
OMIGOD, THAT'S GENTRIFICATION MAN! HE LOOKS BETTER IN PERSON THAN ON HIS INSTAGRAM ACCOUNT.
YEAH, MAYBE HE SHOULD USE A DIFFERENT FILTER.
I'M SORRY THE AESTHETICS OF THIS DISGUSTING STORE, WHICH HAS SERVED THE NEIGHBORHOOD FOR FIVE DECADES, IS VIOLATING YOUR LIFESTYLE.

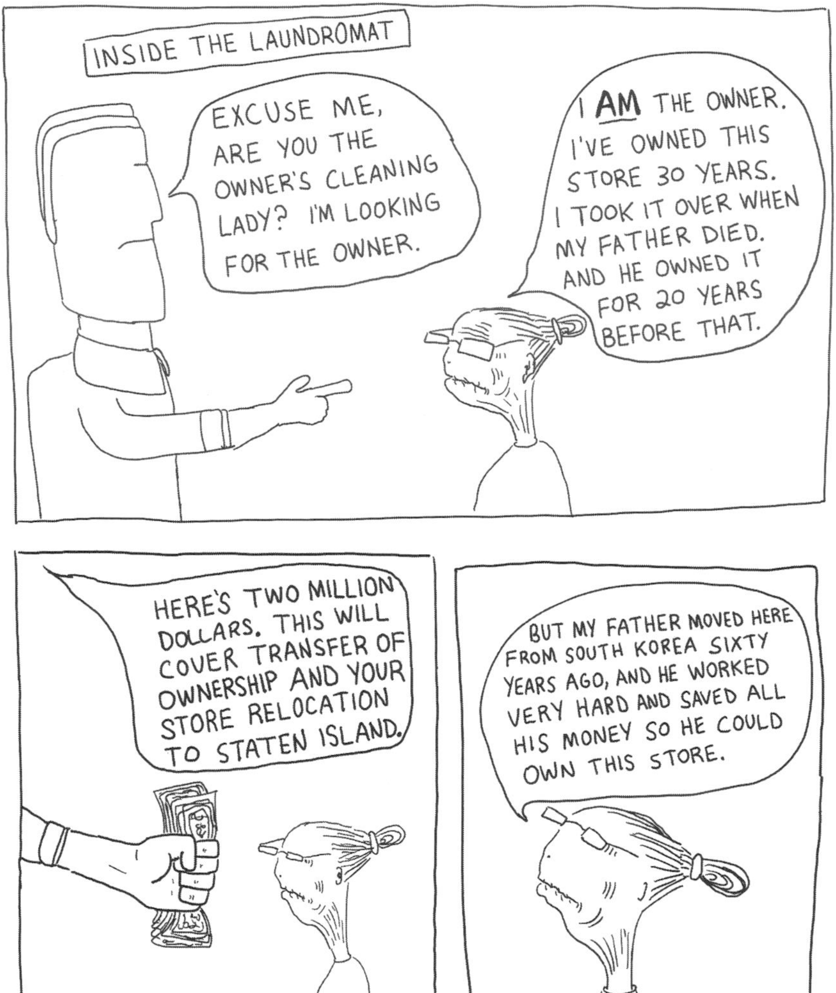
INSIDE THE LAUNDROMAT
EXCUSE ME, ARE YOU THE OWNER'S CLEANING LADY? I'M LOOKING FOR THE OWNER.
I AM THE OWNER. I'VE OWNED THIS STORE 30 YEARS. I TOOK IT OVER WHEN MY FATHER DIED. AND HE OWNED IT FOR 20 YEARS BEFORE THAT.
HERE'S TWO MILLION DOLLARS. THIS WILL COVER TRANSFER OF OWNERSHIP AND YOUR STORE RELOCATION TO STATEN ISLAND.
BUT MY FATHER MOVED HERE FROM SOUTH KOREA SIXTY YEARS AGO, AND HE WORKED VERY HARD AND SAVED ALL HIS MONEY SO HE COULD OWN THIS STORE.

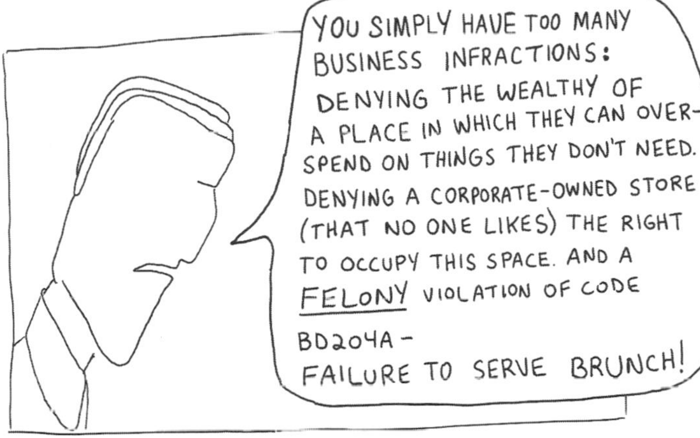
YOU SIMPLY HAVE TOO MANY BUSINESS INFRACTIONS:
DENYING THE WEALTHY OF A PLACE IN WHICH THEY CAN OVER-SPEND ON THINGS THEY DON'T NEED.
DENYING A CORPORATE-OWNED STORE (THAT NO ONE LIKES) THE RIGHT TO OCCUPY THIS SPACE. AND A FELONY VIOLATION OF CODE
BD204A -
FAILURE TO SERVE BRUNCH!

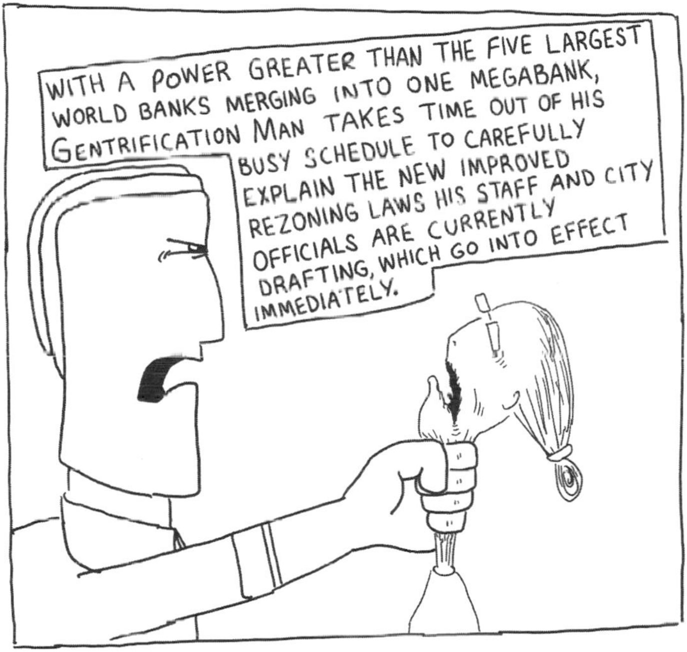
WITH A POWER GREATER THAN THE FIVE LARGEST WORLD BANKS MERGING INTO ONE MEGABANK, GENTRIFICATION MAN TAKES TIME OUT OF HIS BUSY SCHEDULE TO CAREFULLY EXPLAIN THE NEW IMPROVED REZONING LAWS HIS STAFF AND CITY OFFICIALS ARE CURRENTLY DRAFTING, WHICH GO INTO EFFECT IMMEDIATELY.

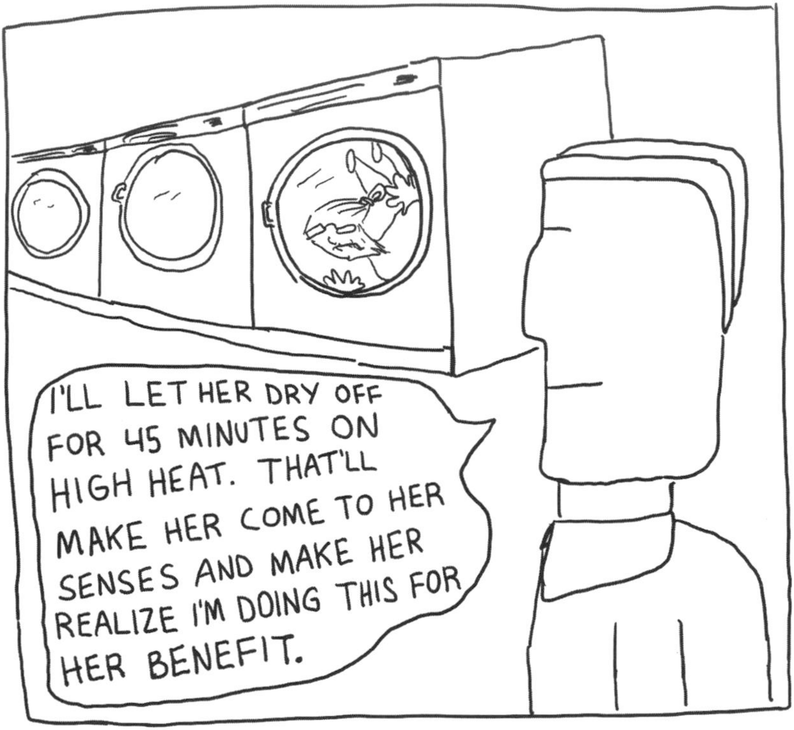
I'LL LET HER DRY OFF FOR 45 MINUTES ON HIGH HEAT. THAT'LL MAKE HER COME TO HER SENSES AND MAKE HER REALIZE I'M DOING THIS FOR HER BENEFIT.

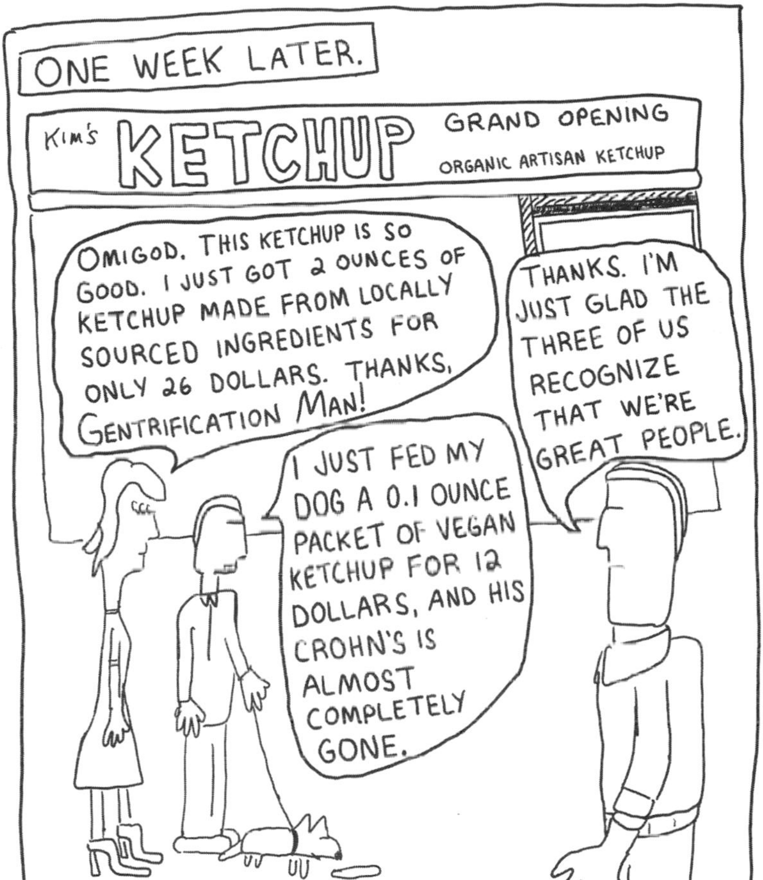
ONE WEEK LATER.
KIM'S KETCHUP GRAND OPENING
ORGANIC ARTISAN KETCHUP
OMIGOD. THIS KETCHUP IS SO GOOD. I JUST GOT 2 OUNCES OF KETCHUP MADE FROM LOCALLY SOURCED INGREDIENTS FOR ONLY 26 DOLLARS. THANKS, GENTRIFICATION MAN!
I JUST FED MY DOG A 0.1 OUNCE PACKET OF VEGAN KETCHUP FOR 12 DOLLARS, AND HIS CROHN'S IS ALMOST COMPLETELY GONE.
THANKS. I'M JUST GLAD THE THREE OF US RECOGNIZE THAT WE'RE GREAT PEOPLE.

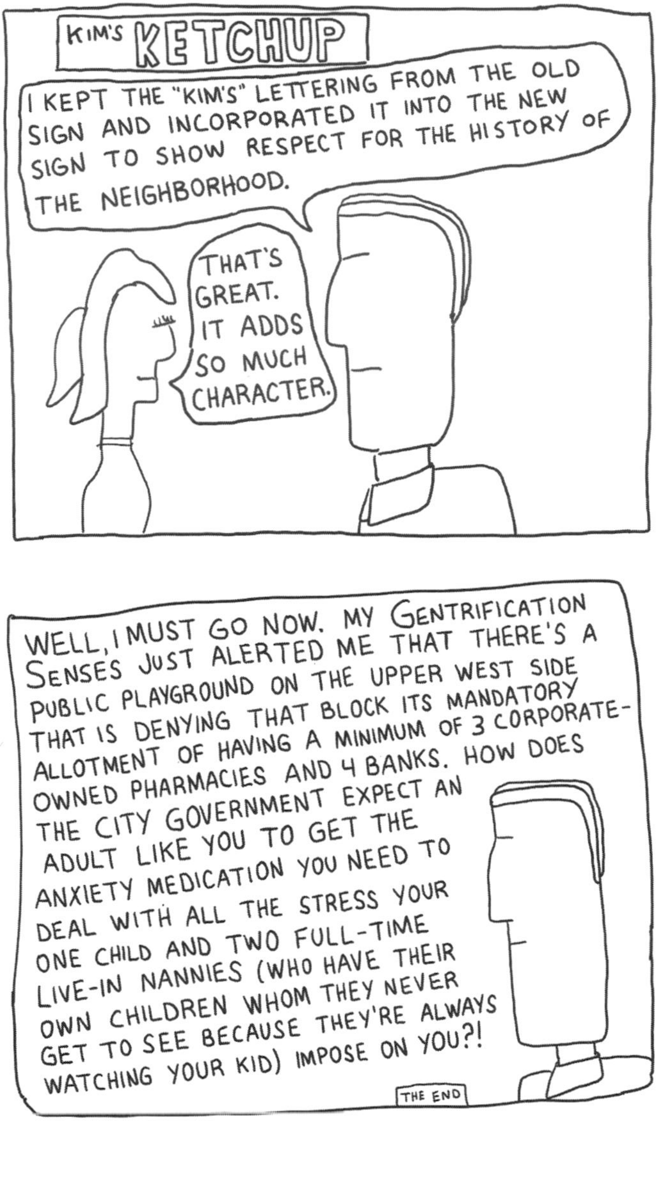
KIM'S KETCHUP
I KEPT THE "KIM'S" LETTERING FROM THE OLD SIGN AND INCORPORATED IT INTO THE NEW SIGN TO SHOW RESPECT FOR THE HISTORY OF THE NEIGHBORHOOD.
THAT'S GREAT. IT ADDS SO MUCH CHARACTER.
WELL, I MUST GO NOW. MY GENTRIFICATION SENSES JUST ALERTED ME THAT THERE'S A PUBLIC PLAYGROUND ON THE UPPER WEST SIDE THAT IS DENYING THAT BLOCK ITS MANDATORY ALLOTMENT OF HAVING A MINIMUM OF 3 CORPORATE-OWNED PHARMACIES AND 4 BANKS. HOW DOES THE CITY GOVERNMENT EXPECT AN ADULT LIKE YOU TO GET THE ANXIETY MEDICATION YOU NEED TO DEAL WITH ALL THE STRESS YOUR ONE CHILD AND TWO FULL-TIME LIVE-IN NANNIES (WHO HAVE THEIR OWN CHILDREN WHOM THEY NEVER GET TO SEE BECAUSE THEY'RE ALWAYS WATCHING YOUR KID) IMPOSE ON YOU?!
THE END

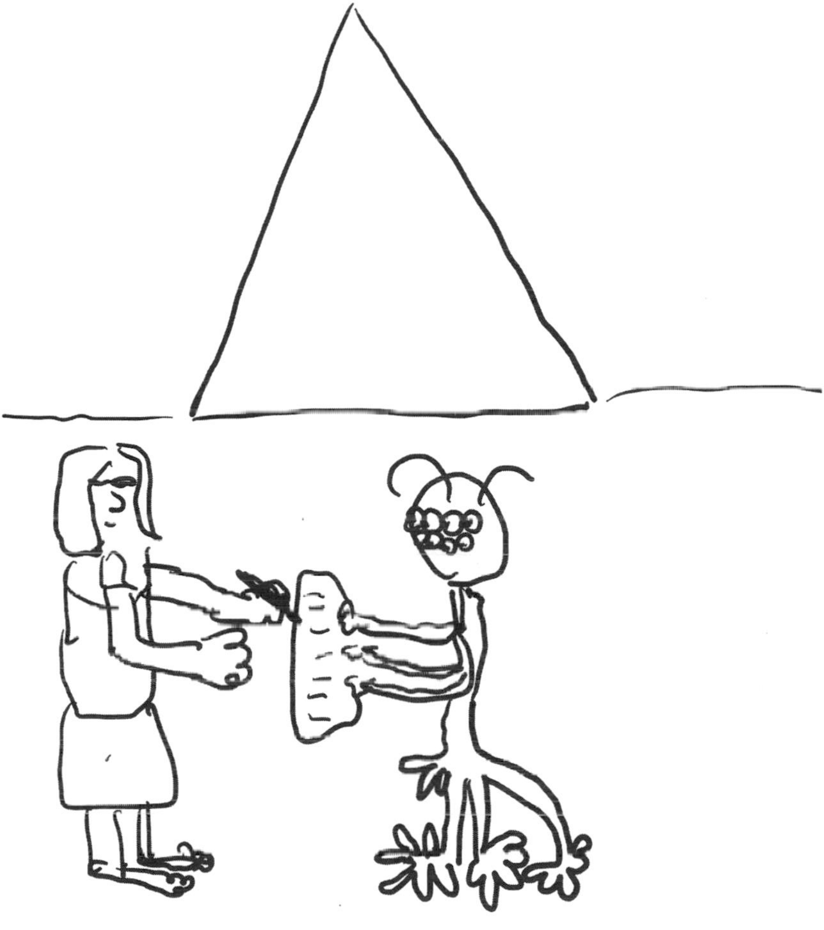

Pharaoh signing paperwork for delivery of the first pyramid.

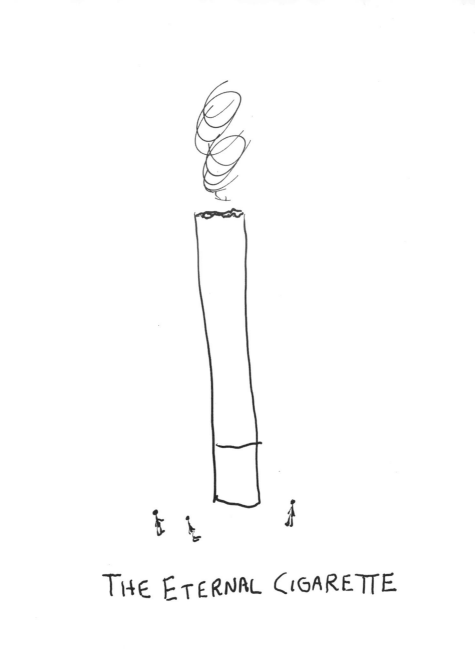

THE ETERNAL CIGARETTE

TUG OF WILL

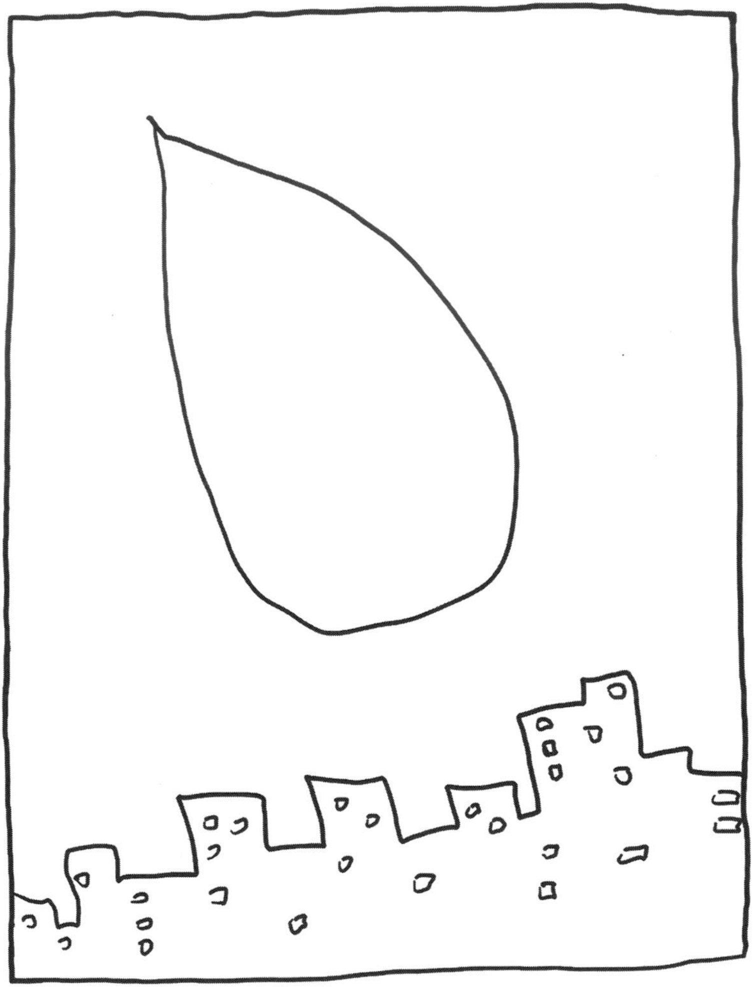

If the raindrops united.

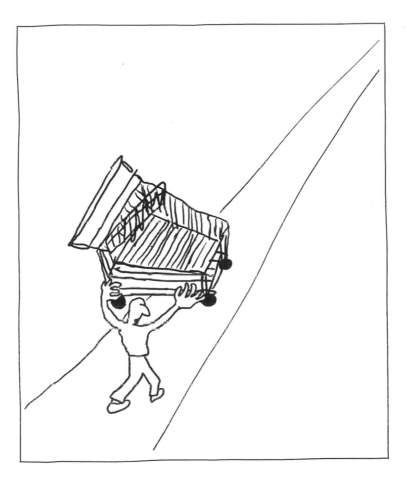

NOVICE SHOPPING CART THIEF

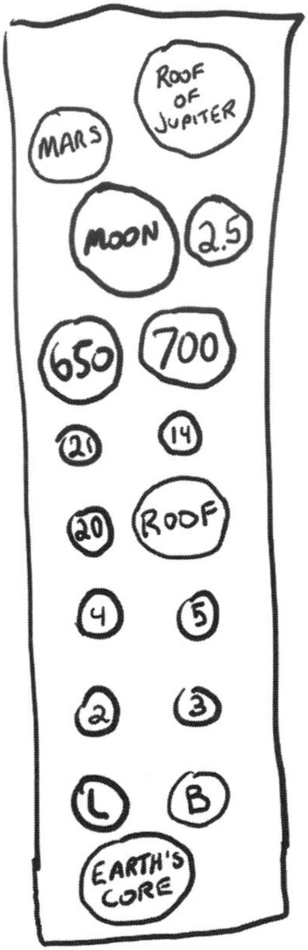
ROOF OF JUPITER
MARS
MOON
2.5
650
700
21
14
20
ROOF
4
5
2
3
L
B
EARTH'S CORE

MY ELEVATOR

The alphabet before it got its act together.

BY 2075, 80% OF PEOPLE HAD THEIR NOSES
SURGICALLY REPLACED WITH DIGITAL CLOCKS.

WITH HIGH LEVELS OF POLLUTION, THE SENSE OF SMELL BECAME SOMETHING MOST HUMANS WISHED THEY NEVER HAD. AS HUMANS GOT WORSE AT NON-COMPUTER-AIDED REAL LIFE DIRECT HUMAN-TO-HUMAN SPEECH COMMUNICATION, THE VAST MAJORITY NEEDED ARTIFICIAL ASSISTANCE TO INITIATE CONVERSATION.

THERE WAS NO OFFICIAL LAW REQUIRING THE REMOVAL OF NOSES AND THE WEARING OF FACECLOCKS. BUT IT BECAME SO COMMONPLACE, THAT IF YOU DID NOT GET THE NOSE REMOVAL/FACECLOCK PROCEDURE, IT BECAME NEARLY IMPOSSIBLE TO HAVE A CONVERSATION WITH ANYONE. WHAT THE PEOPLE DID NOT KNOW WAS THAT WHEN THEIR NOSES WERE REMOVED, 100% OF THEM WERE IMPLANTED WITH TRACKING DEVICES BY THE GOVERNMENT. ALL OF THE FACECLOCKS HAD MIND AND MOOD CONTROL TECHNOLOGY - WHICH WAS ALSO BIOLOGICALLY ADDICTING - WHICH MADE PEOPLE NEVER EVEN HAVE THE DESIRE TO REMOVE THE FACECLOCKS.

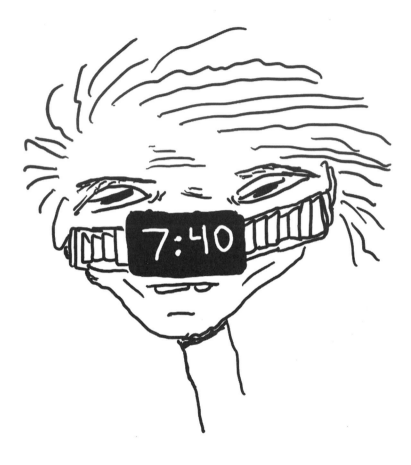

TO KEEP THE FACECLOCKS CHARGED, MONTHLY FEES HAD TO BE PAID TO THE GOVERNMENT (WHICH WAS OWNED BY THE CORPORATION). THE GENERAL PUBLIC CALLED THESE DEVICES "FACECLOCKS." THE GOVERNMENT/CORPORATION SECRETLY CALLED THIS "OPERATION FACE WATCH."

TOES MEET WHERE THEY COME FROM

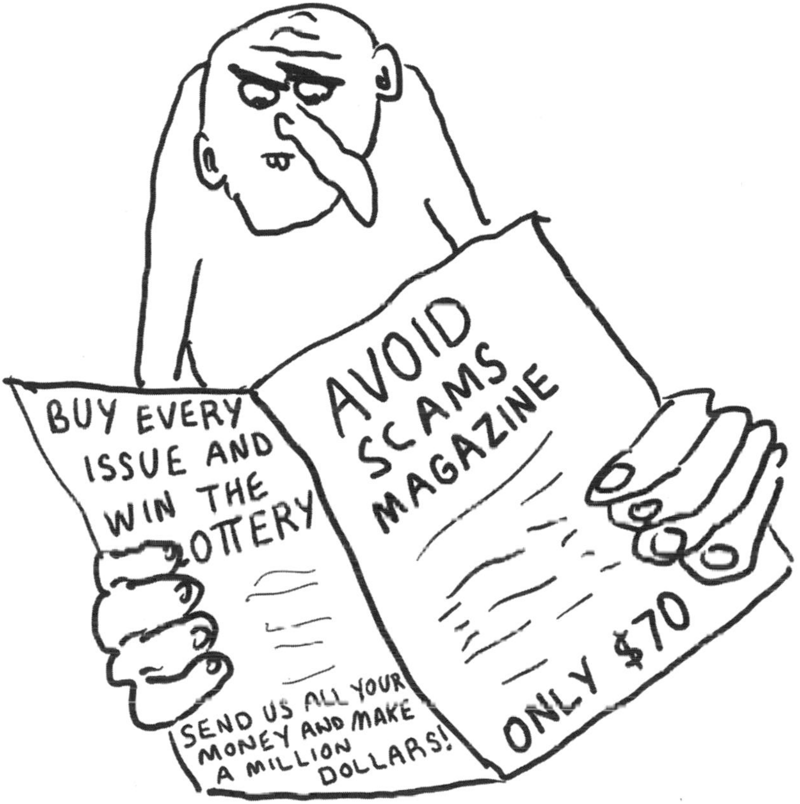
BUY EVERY ISSUE AND WIN THE LOTTERY
SEND US ALL YOUR MONEY AND MAKE A MILLION DOLLARS!
AVOID SCAMS MAGAZINE
ONLY $70

People Who Can Read My Handwriting

People Who Can't Read My Handwriting

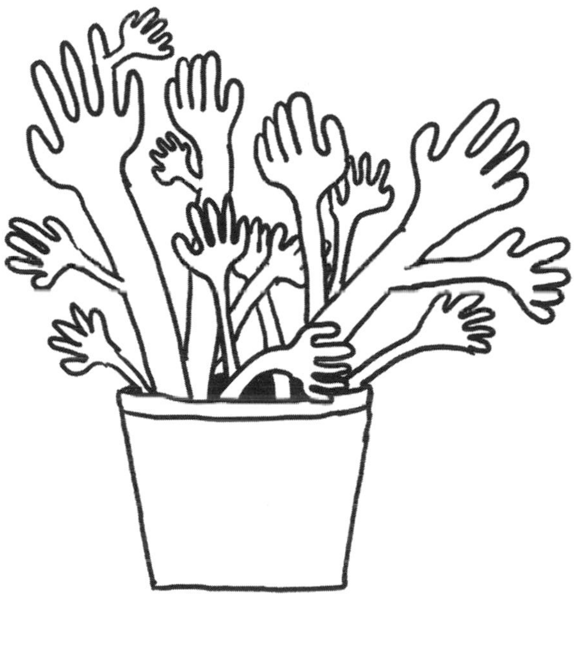

HIGH FIVE PLANT

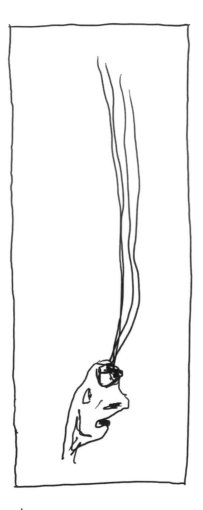

NORD'S CLASSMATES MADE FUN OF HIM BECAUSE HE WAS SHORT, HAD A WEIRD NAME, AND HAD VERY LONG EYELASHES.

WHEN IT RAINED, HIS EYELASHES WOULD
OBSCURE HIS VISION AND COVER HIS FEET.

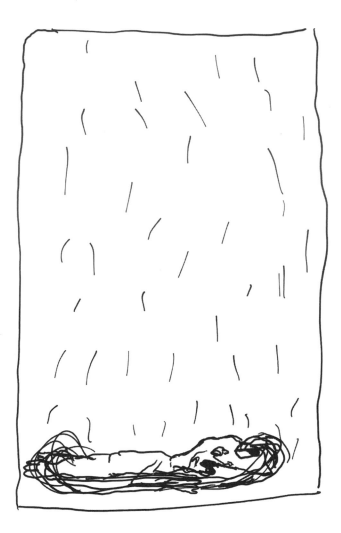

USUALLY CAUSING HIM TO TRIP AND FALL.

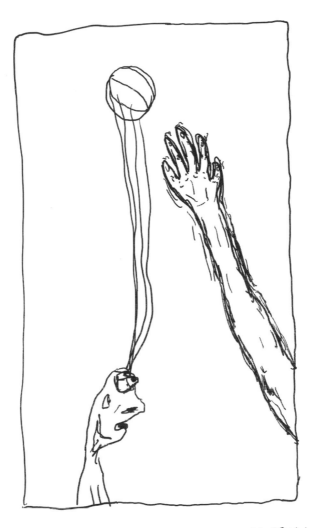

BUT HE WAS GREAT AT BASKETBALL.

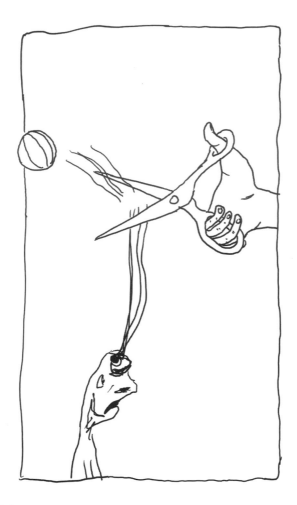

UNLESS THE OTHER TEAM HAD SCISSORS.
AND THAT'S WHY SCISSORS WERE BANNED
FROM BASKETBALL IN 1926.

PUNISHMENT FOR NOT PAYING RENT ON TIME

COCKROACH ON STILTS IS PREPARED FOR RISING SEA LEVELS.

PARTIAL HISTORY OF THE TWENTY DOLLAR BILL

For years, the twenty dollar bill was just like all the other bills.

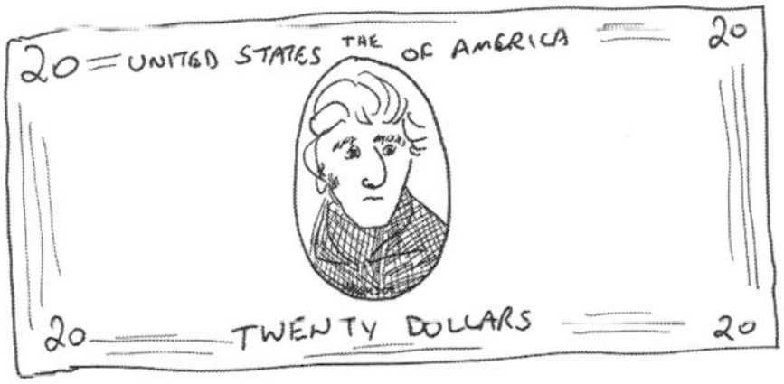
20
UNITED STATES THE OF AMERICA
TWENTY DOLLARS

Then in 1998, it got a big head.

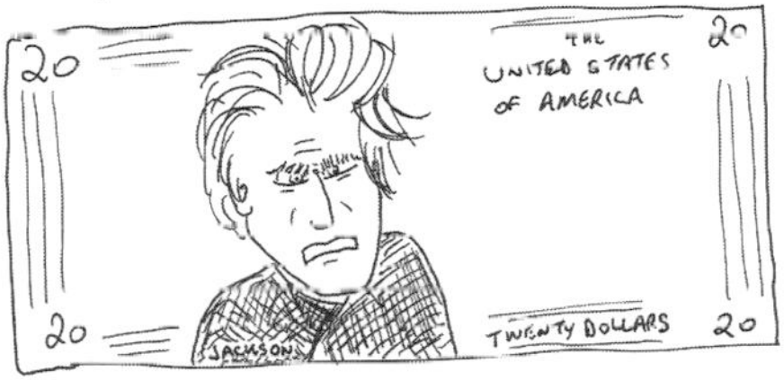
20
THE UNITED STATES OF AMERICA
TWENTY DOLLARS
JACKSON

By 2024, it got out of control.

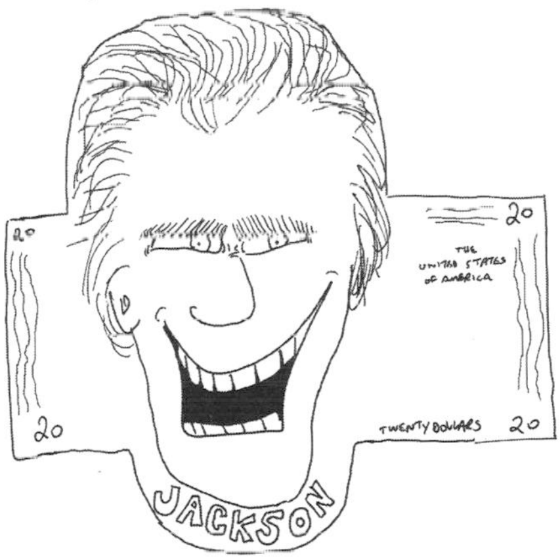
20
THE UNITED STATES OF AMERICA
TWENTY DOLLARS
JACKSON

POPULAR LIFE FORM YEAR 2250

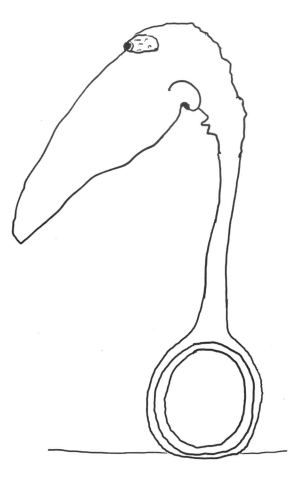

No eyelids.
So it can absorb information 24 hours a day.

Large nose.
So it can more rapidly smell pollution - which is its main source of energy - of which there is an unlimited supply.

No hair.
Hair vanished from society in 2245 when it was declared illegal. Hair would get dirty from pollution. Pollution stuck in hair was considered a waste because that pollution otherwise could've been nasally inhaled to power the life forms. Hair was also banned because it was often used to reflect mood and personality.

No arms.
Arms are unnecessary because it comes with apps that take care of everything.

No ears.
Listening to another life form is a felony since it is considered to be anti-narcissistic and a weapon of communism.

ARMPIT HAIR SALON

ROLLERCOASTER FOR WIMPS

NOSE JOB #35

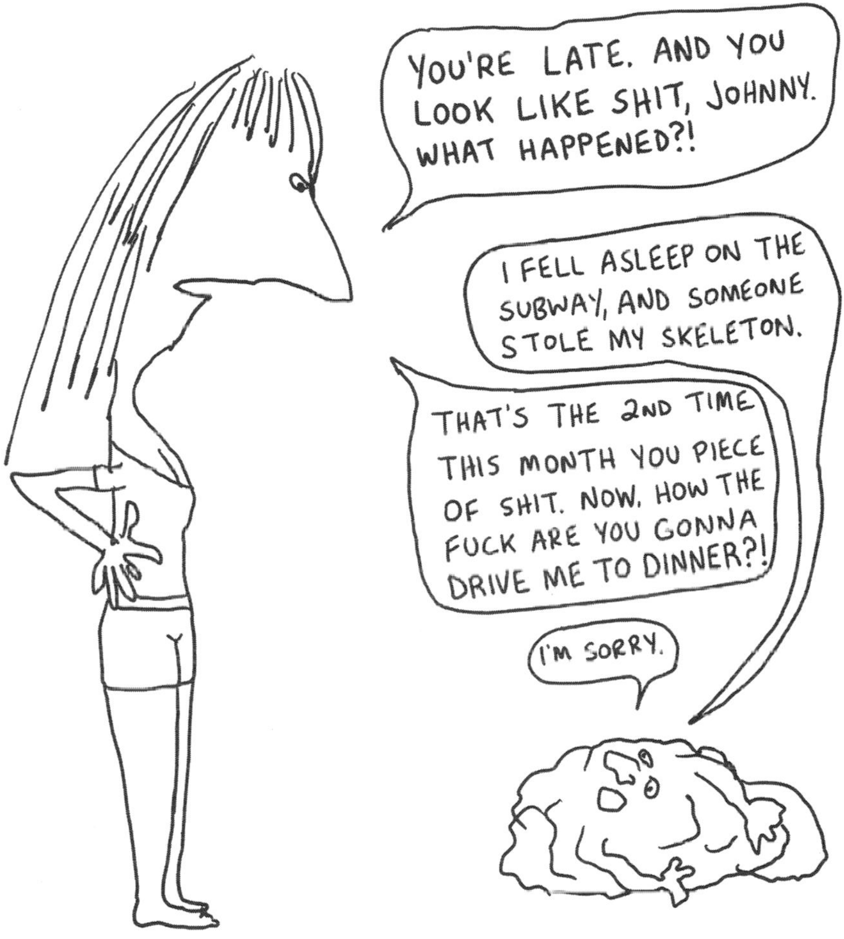
YOU'RE LATE. AND YOU LOOK LIKE SHIT, JOHNNY. WHAT HAPPENED?!
I FELL ASLEEP ON THE SUBWAY, AND SOMEONE STOLE MY SKELETON.
THAT'S THE 2ND TIME THIS MONTH YOU PIECE OF SHIT. NOW, HOW THE FUCK ARE YOU GONNA DRIVE ME TO DINNER?!
I'M SORRY.

Billy listens to his neighbors, who live on the opposite side of the page, have an argument.

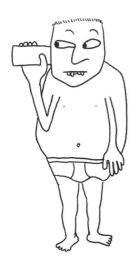

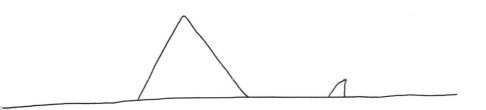

PYRAMID   VS   SHARK

NEW TREE STRATEGY

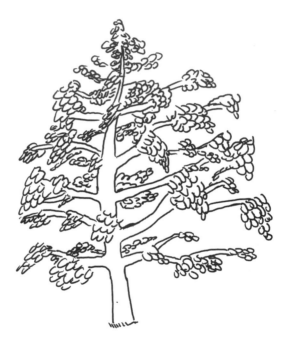

WINTER: WEAR LEAVES TO STAY WARM

NEW TREE STRATEGY

SUMMER: REMOVE LEAVES TO COOL OFF

Jeff
"Swiss Cheese
Teeth"
Johnson

PYRAMID SCHEMING

A M P U T E E

On Kenny's 35th birthday, his parents discovered
he was a music prodigy.

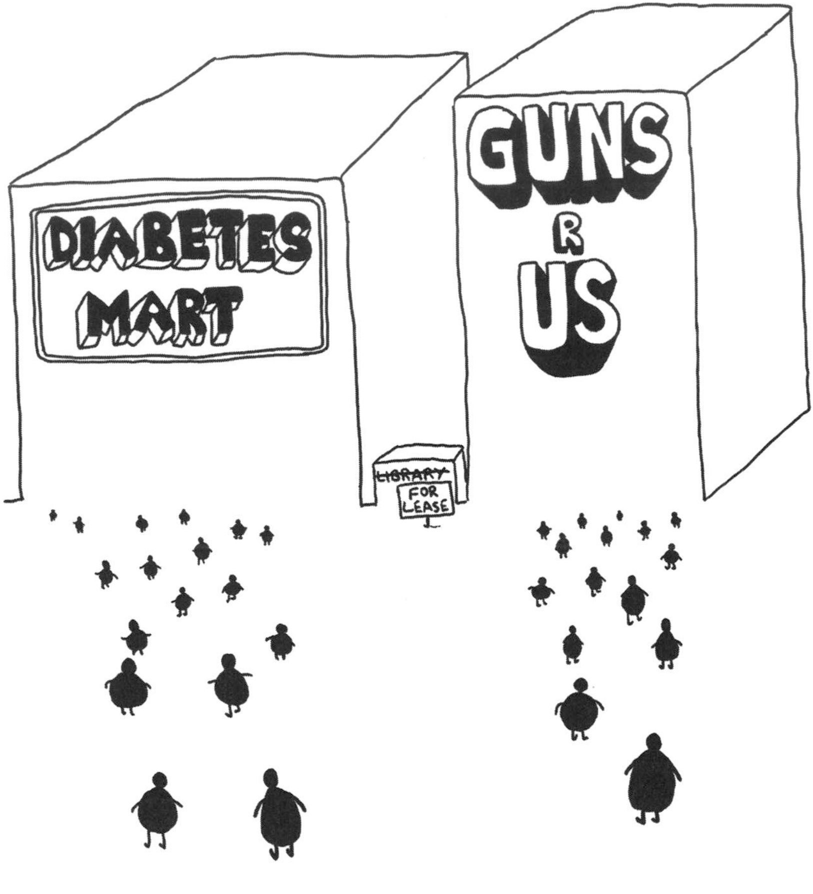
DIABETES MART
GUNS R US
LIBRARY
FOR LEASE

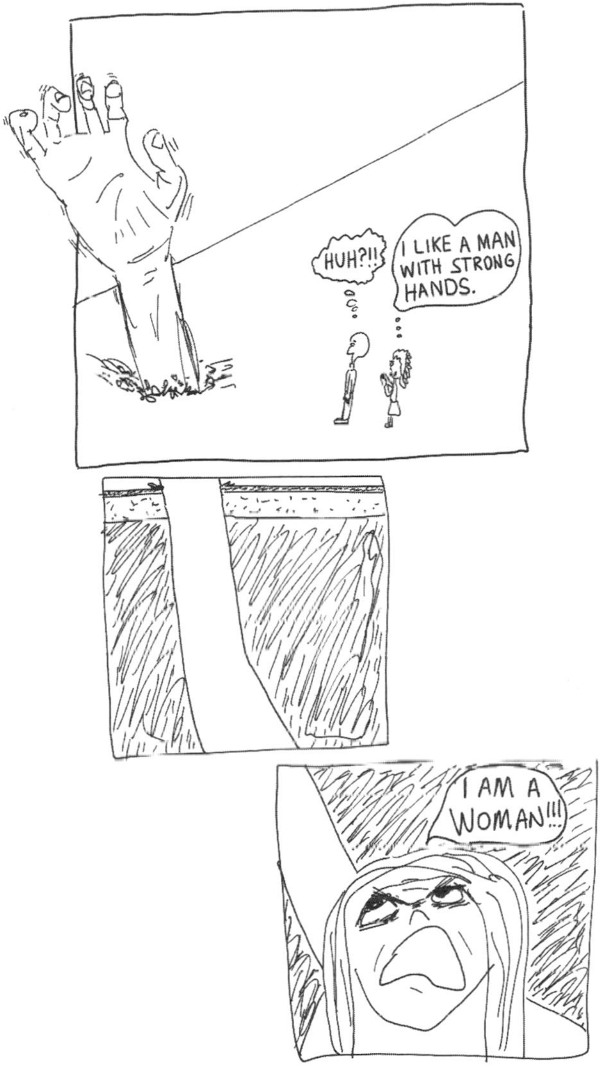
HUH?!!
I LIKE A MAN WITH STRONG HANDS.
I AM A WOMAN!!!

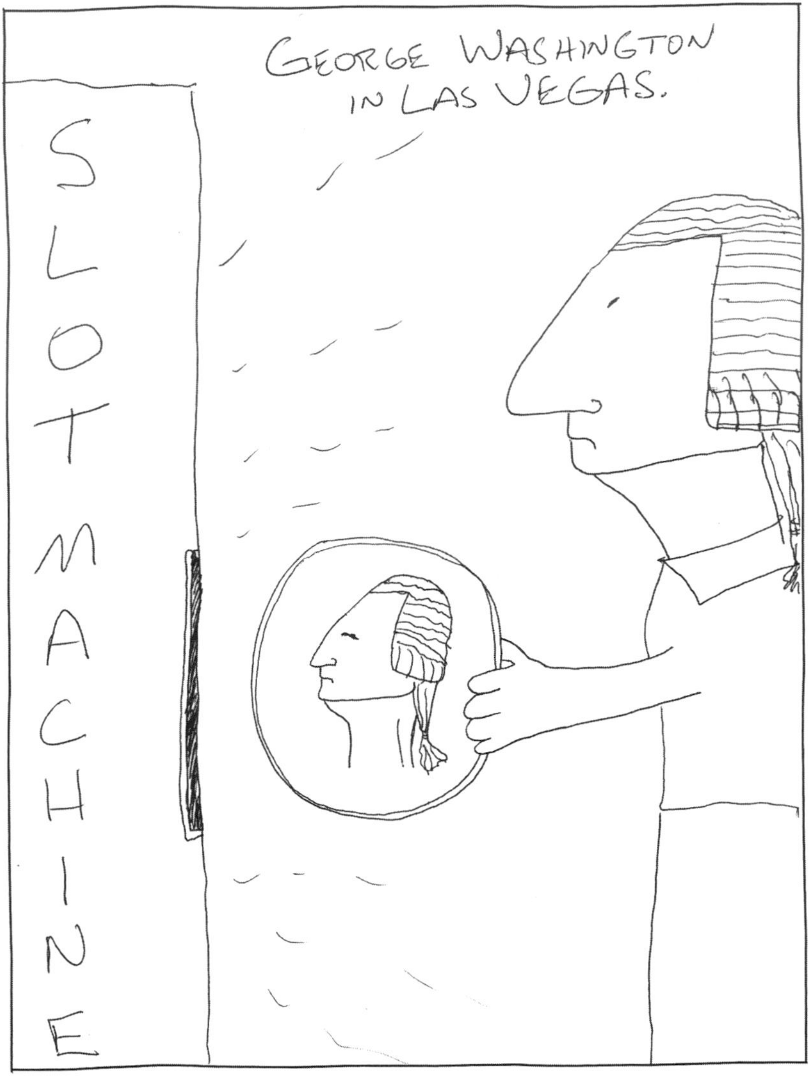
GEORGE WASHINGTON IN LAS VEGAS.
SLOT MACHINE

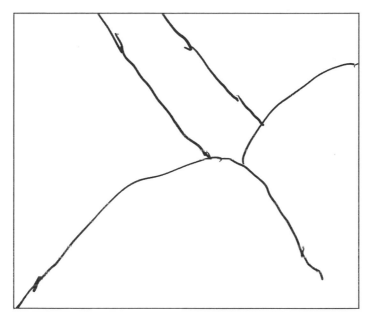

Keystone Pipeline going through America.

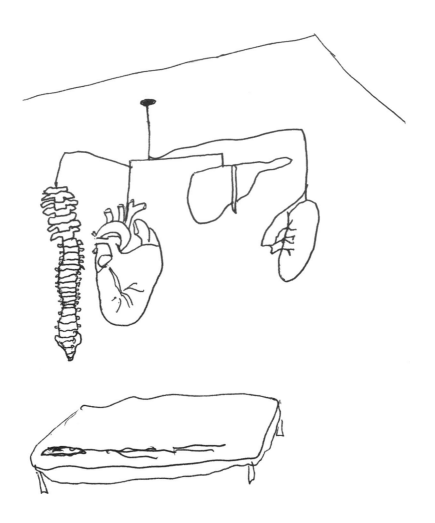

ORGAN MOBILE AND HOSPITAL PATIENT

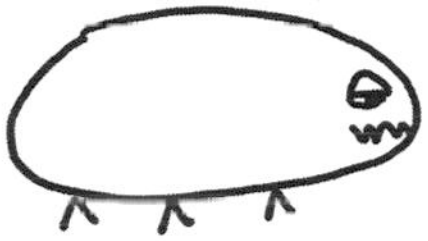

TICK

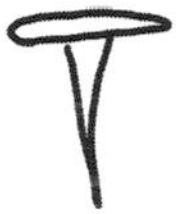

TACK

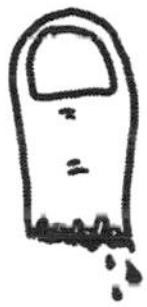

TOE

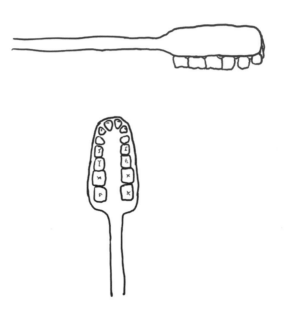

TEETHBRUSHES

DON'T BOTHER TRYING TO FIND YOUR INNER CHILD.
IT'S BUSY TEXTING, AND IT DOESN'T WANT TO
TALK TO YOU.

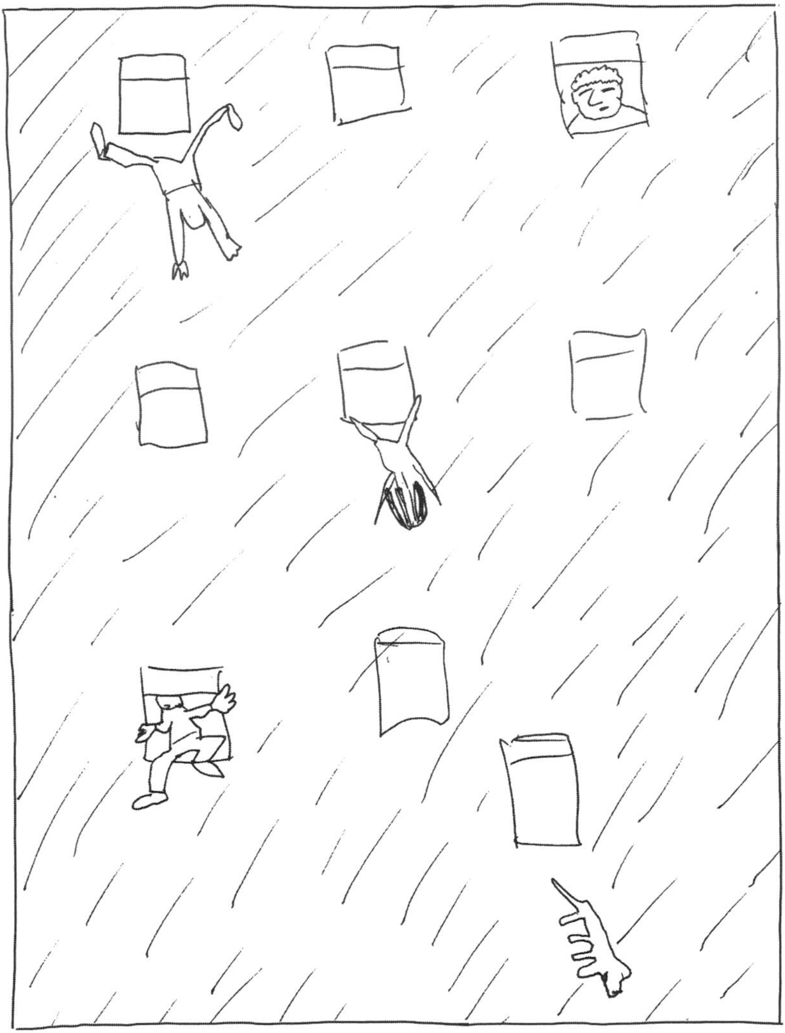

BILLY WATCHES HIS BUILDING'S SEMI-ANNUAL SUICIDE RACE.

ANNA'S SUBWAY SALE

THE NYC BUILDING BASKETBALL TEAM
STARTING LINEUP

1   2   3   4   5

① Empire State Building at center.
② Chrysler Building - power forword
③ Woolworth Building - small forword
④ Marcy Projects - shooting guard
⑤ The Spinolas' attached house in Queens -
                    point guard

Norman drinks his
daily plate of
fresh brain juice.

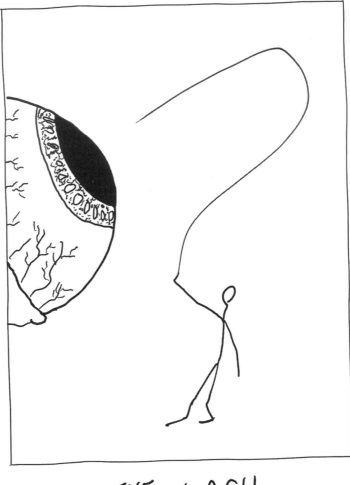

EYE LASH

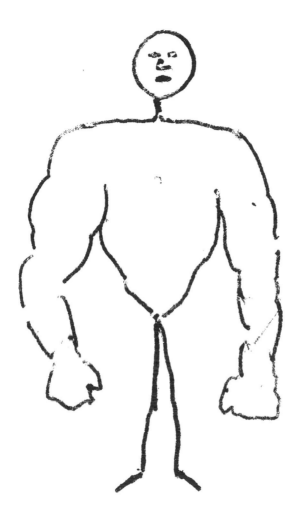

Always work out your whole body.

CRIMES AGAINST ICE CREAM

PEPPERONI VANILLA WITH
CHEESE WIZ ON TOP

NEW YORK, NEW YORK

SPEED BANK
PHARMACY
OTHER PHARMACY
GLOBAL BANK
EVERYWHERE BANK
PHARMACY EXPRESS
SAME PHARMACY AS 5 DOORS DOWN
UNIVERSAL BANK

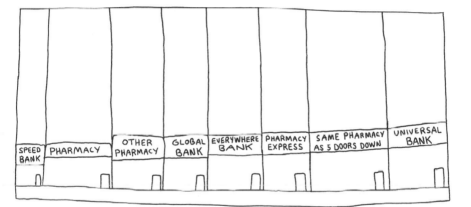

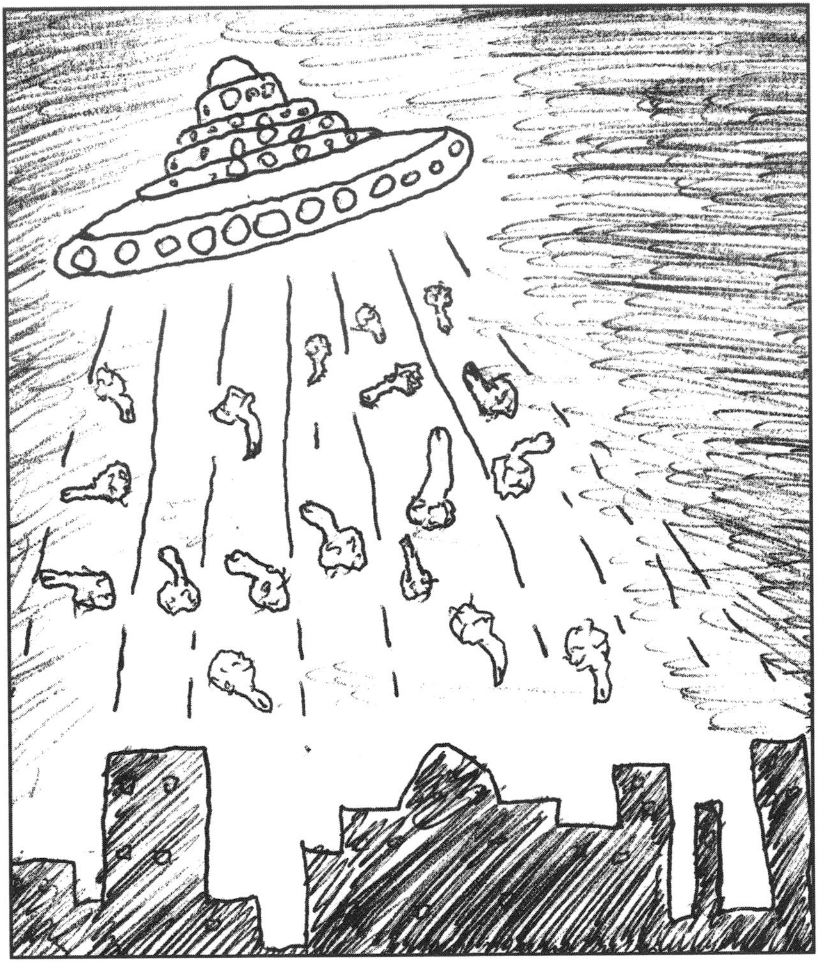

And the next morning, all the male genitalia were gone.

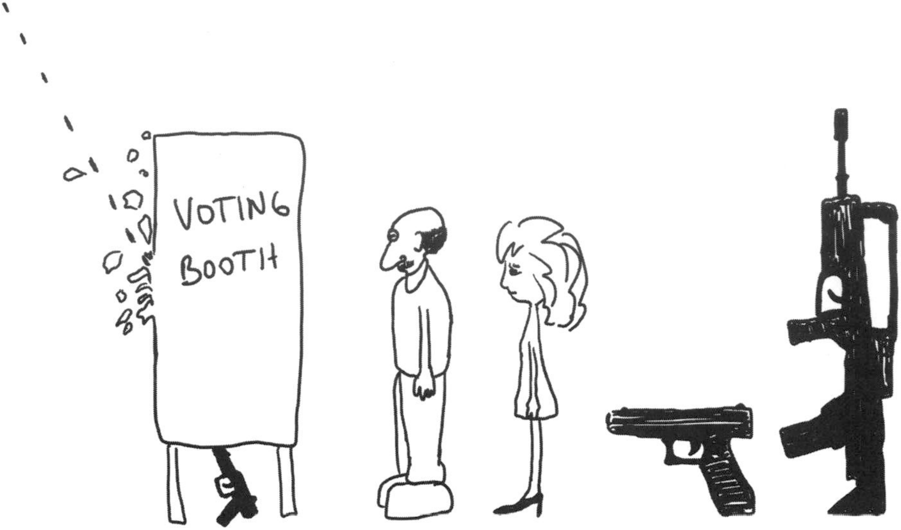
VOTING
BOOTH

In 2050, guns got the right to vote.

They would cast their vote by shooting the name of the candidate they did <u>not</u> like.

On a sunny day from the White House lawn in 2058,
the President gives a speech assuring America
that it does not have a pollution problem.

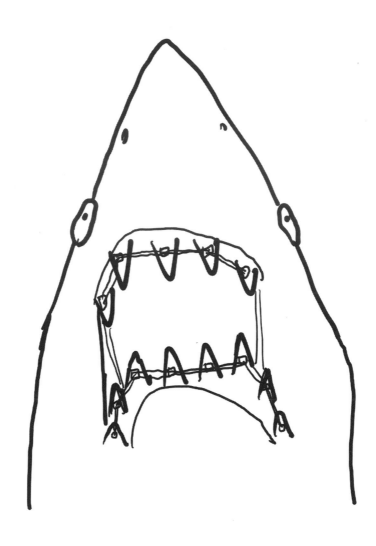

TEENAGE SHARK

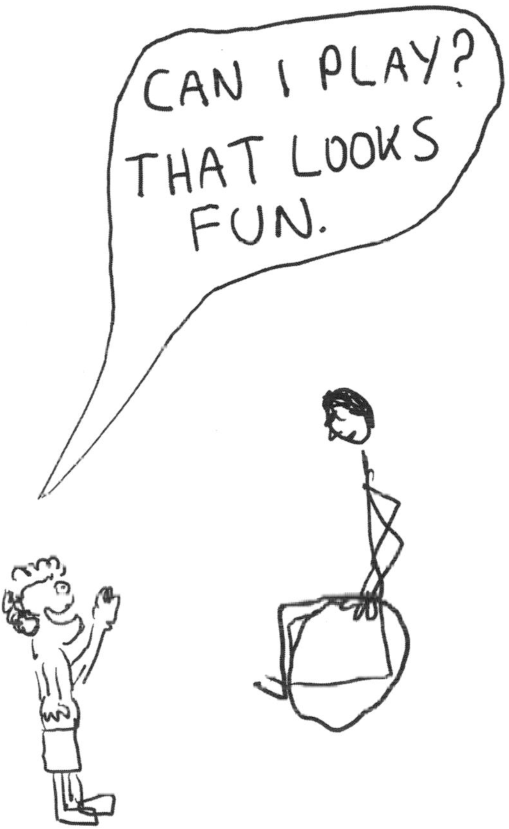
CAN I PLAY? THAT LOOKS FUN.

Six-year-old Bobby before he learned that the wheelchair is not a toy.

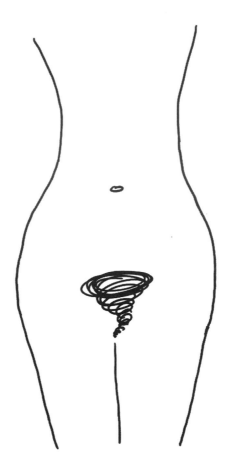

TORNADO

SCARF

This is the last photo ever taken of the Watsons and their six adopted children. Leonard, the tallest of their children, was the first to get caught in the giant spiderweb and never escape. Only the Watsons' dog, Gerald, survived.

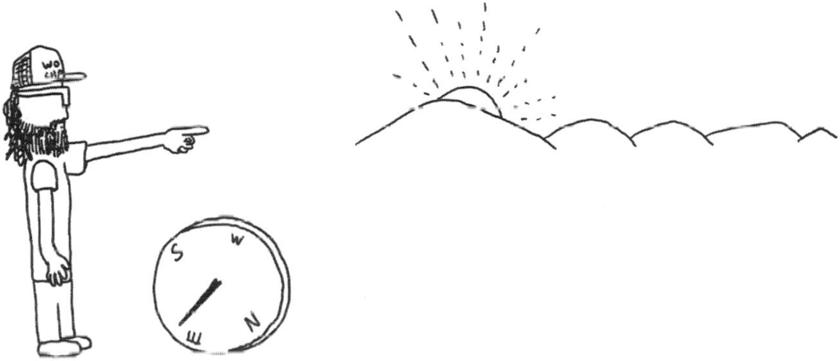
S
W
N
E

ME GIVING DIRECTIONS TO A COMPASS.

Hug a corporation. Corporations are people too.

IN 2290, DAILY LIFE BECAME SO MONOTONOUS,
HUMANOIDS WOULD INSERT ANXIETY CHIPS
SO THEY COULD MOMENTARILY FEEL SOME
KIND OF EMOTION.

IT'S A BICYCLE WITH A TURNTABLE!
COMMUTE AND DJ AT THE SAME TIME!

GREEN ENERGY PRODUCT FOR "COOL" PEOPLE.

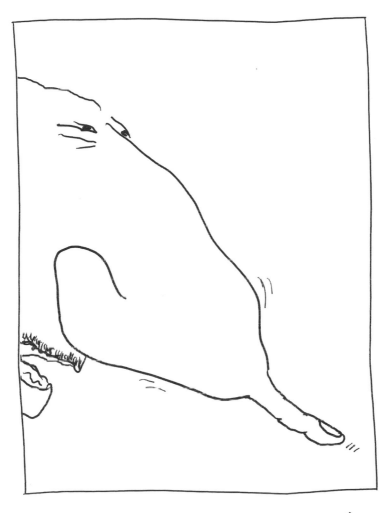

"You! Why are you staring at me?!"

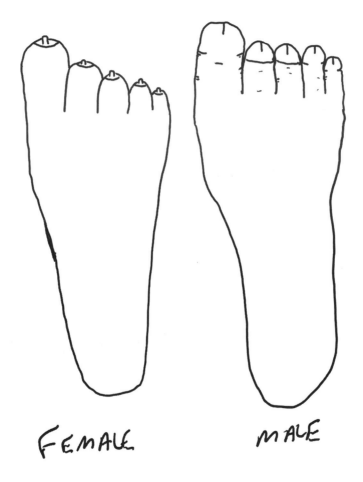

FEMALE   MALE

FULL-TIME

PART-TIME

CALLED-IN-SICK

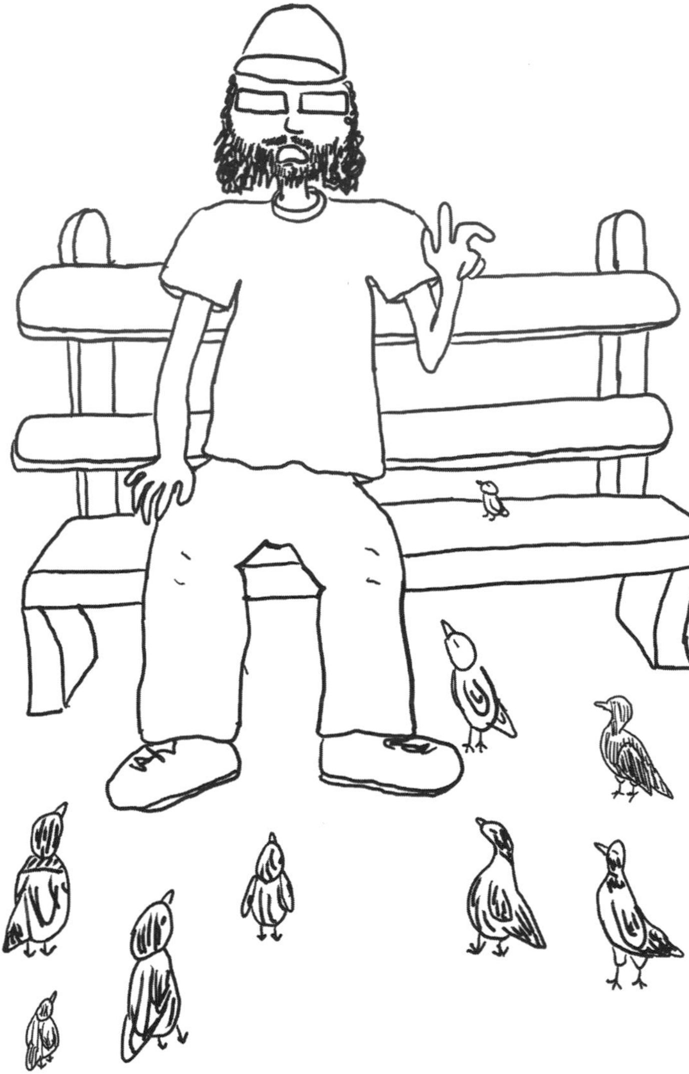

"You think the police are going to continue to leave you alone?! If the government isn't making money off you, they're going to arrest you or kick you out of the city. They're going to ask you if you have I.D. - and you won't have any - and they'll arrest you for loitering. And when they permanently injure you - or kill you while you're in custody - no one will ever know because none of you have cell phones with video cameras. Why?! Because none of you have jobs and you got no money. You used to have jobs as carrier pigeons, but fax machines and email put you out of business. And if you fly to Jersey, you're stuck there because you won't be able to pay the toll to get back! I'm just trying to let you know what's going on. You gotta get video cameras. And think of all the great angles you could get. You could go high up in the air or trees, and the cops would never know you were filming them. Now some cops are cool, but—"

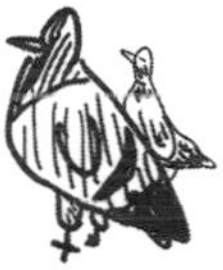

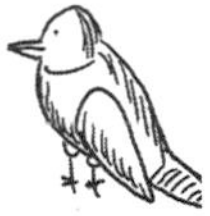

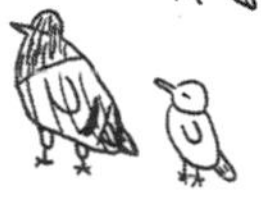

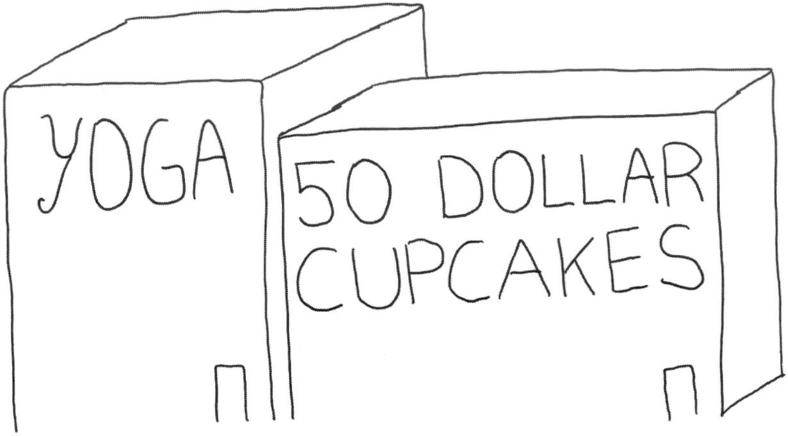
YOGA
50 DOLLAR CUPCAKES

Where to meet women in Manhattan.

UBER TURTLE

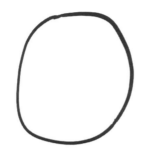

The letter O.

The letter O with bad balance.

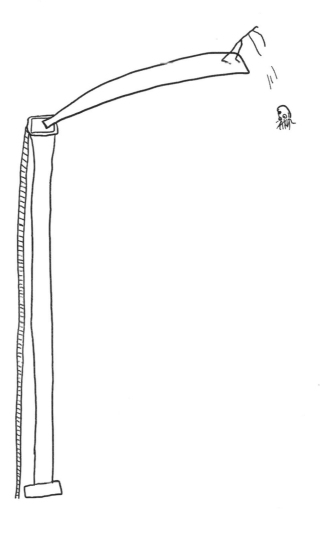

GOTH
CRAYON
BOX

SCHOOL BUS SAFETY IDEA #24

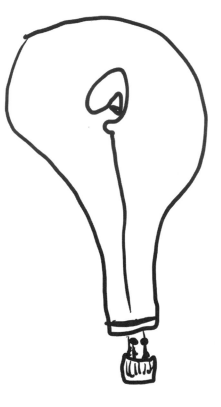

HOT AIR LIGHTBULB

Because his short arms are unable to reach, Jeremy has grown nose twigs to prevent cockroaches from invading his eyes.

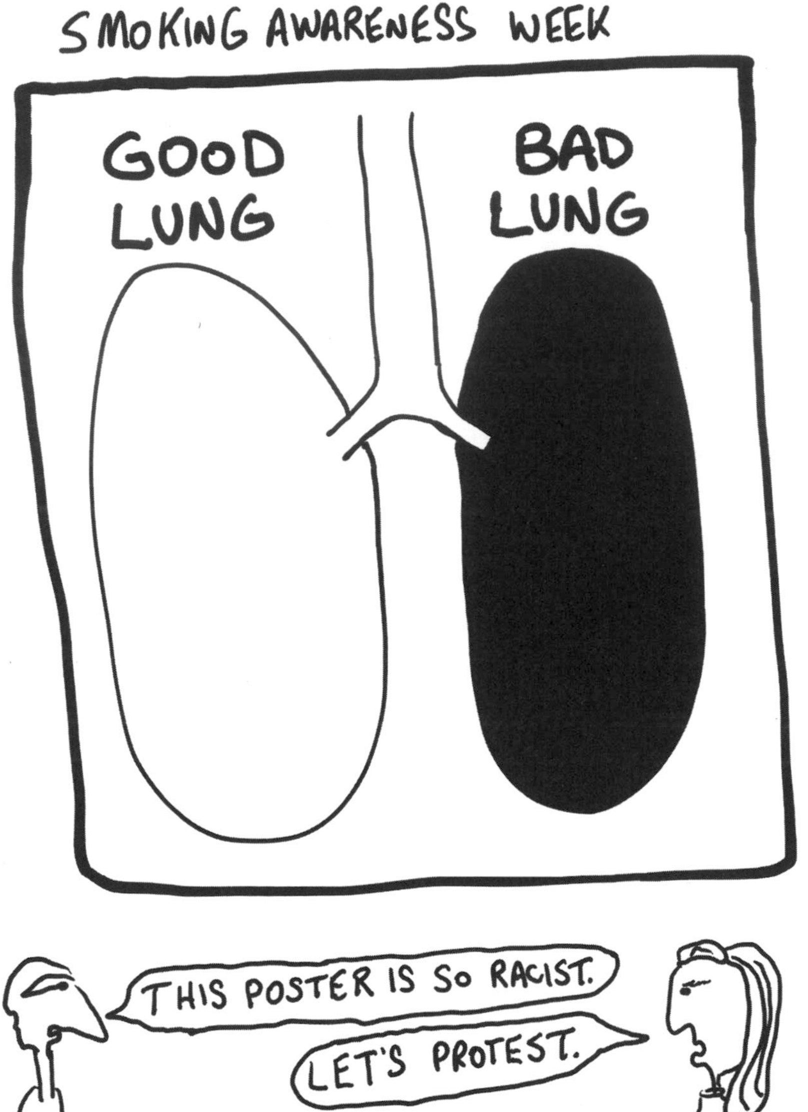
SMOKING AWARENESS WEEK
GOOD LUNG
BAD LUNG
THIS POSTER IS SO RACIST.
LET'S PROTEST.

Save time and comb your entire head with one stroke using the Mastercomb.

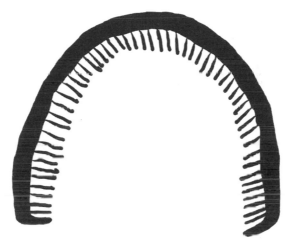

A new way to manage your hair in today's fast-paced world.

Works with any human head.

TOAST FACE

POWER

POWERED
DOWN

CONTROLLED
POWER

HIDDEN
POWER

NO
POWER

ANTI-VAXXER RATTLESNAKE

"I'm not anti-science, I'm just pro-diseases' rights."

Fred, The Talking Parrot, bores Richard,
The Listening Cockroach.

NOSE JOB #43

The nose is good for taking a nap because
it is dark, warm, moist, and soft. With its
two nostrils, the nose is a bunk bed for
people who fear ladders.

WARNING: DO NOT SLEEP IN NOSE IF IT HAS A SINUS INFECTION.

THINGS SHIPS COLLECT

EXAMPLE #1

BANKER IN A BOTTLE

A QUESTION MARK GAINS CONFIDENCE

SEESAWED OFF

And one day, the Chrysler Building decided
it had had enough of NYC.

In 2071, lobbyists for developers were successful in passing a new law that made it a felony for trees to litter. That fall, the last 200 trees left in America were incarcerated.

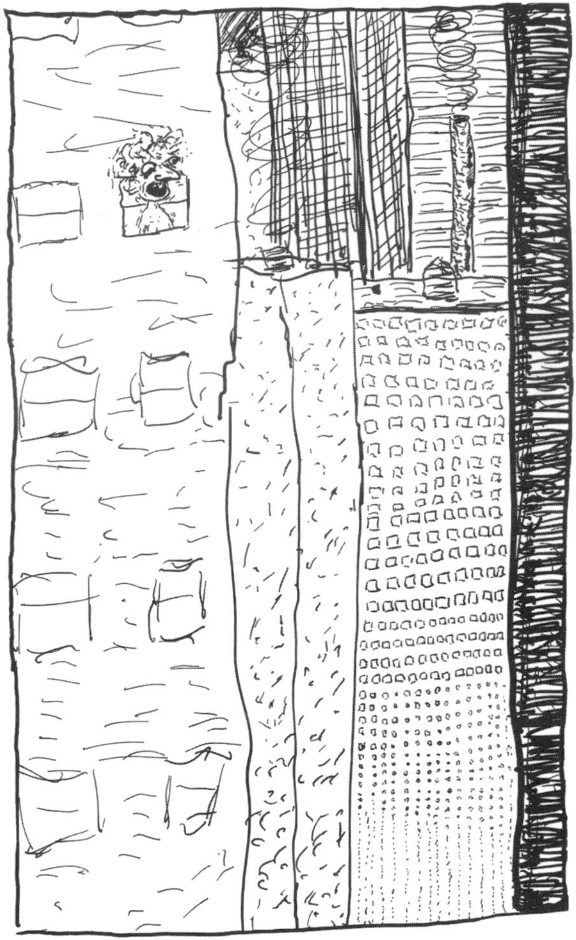

"Fuck you, midtown!!!" he cried for hours and hours as no one listened.

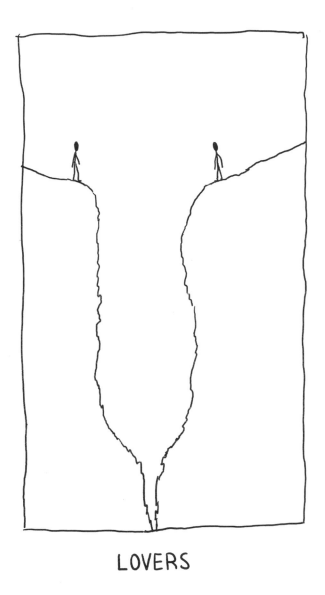

LOVERS

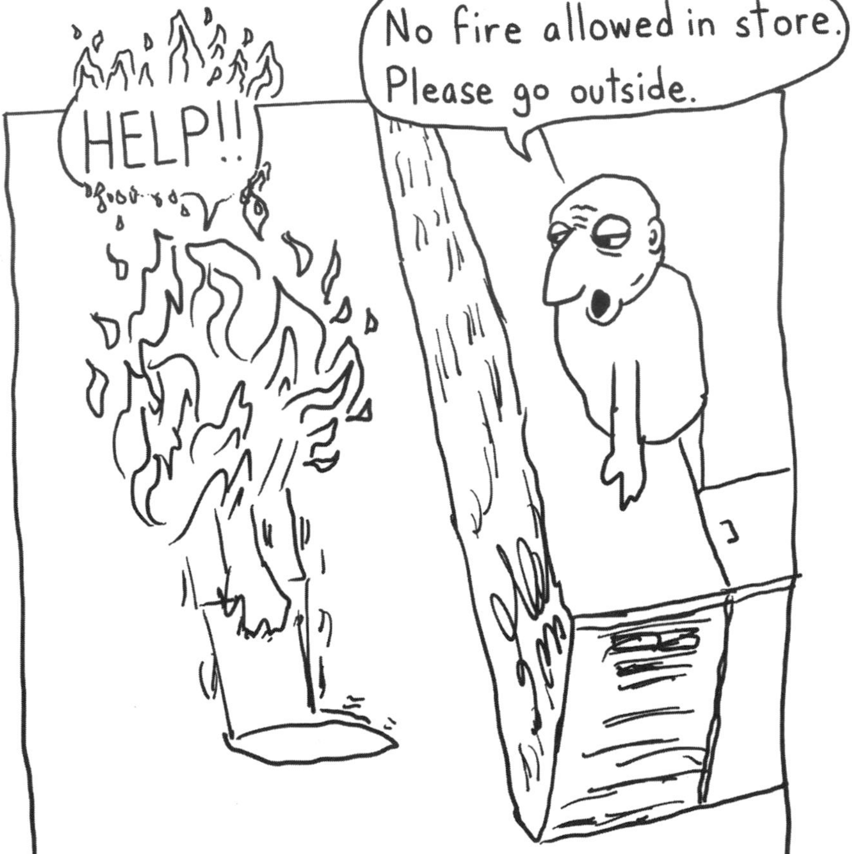
HELP!!
No fire allowed in store. Please go outside.

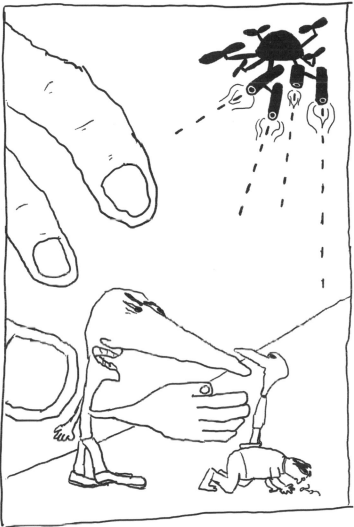

HUMANITY

PRESIDENT'S SON KILLS A RAINBOW

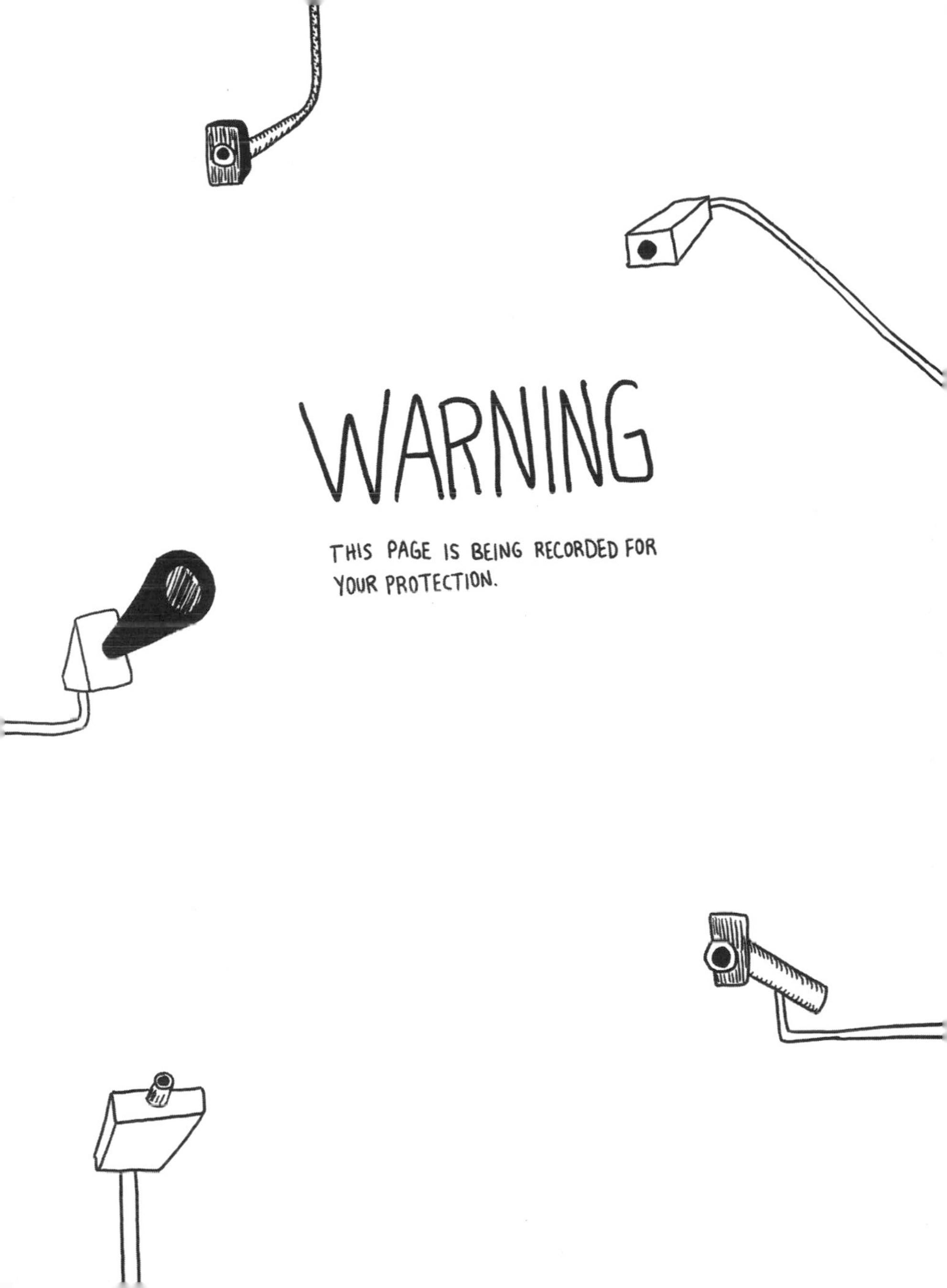
WARNING
THIS PAGE IS BEING RECORDED FOR YOUR PROTECTION.

SAVE PAPER

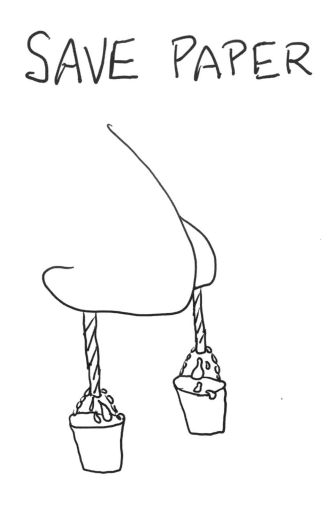

USE SNOT CATCHERS

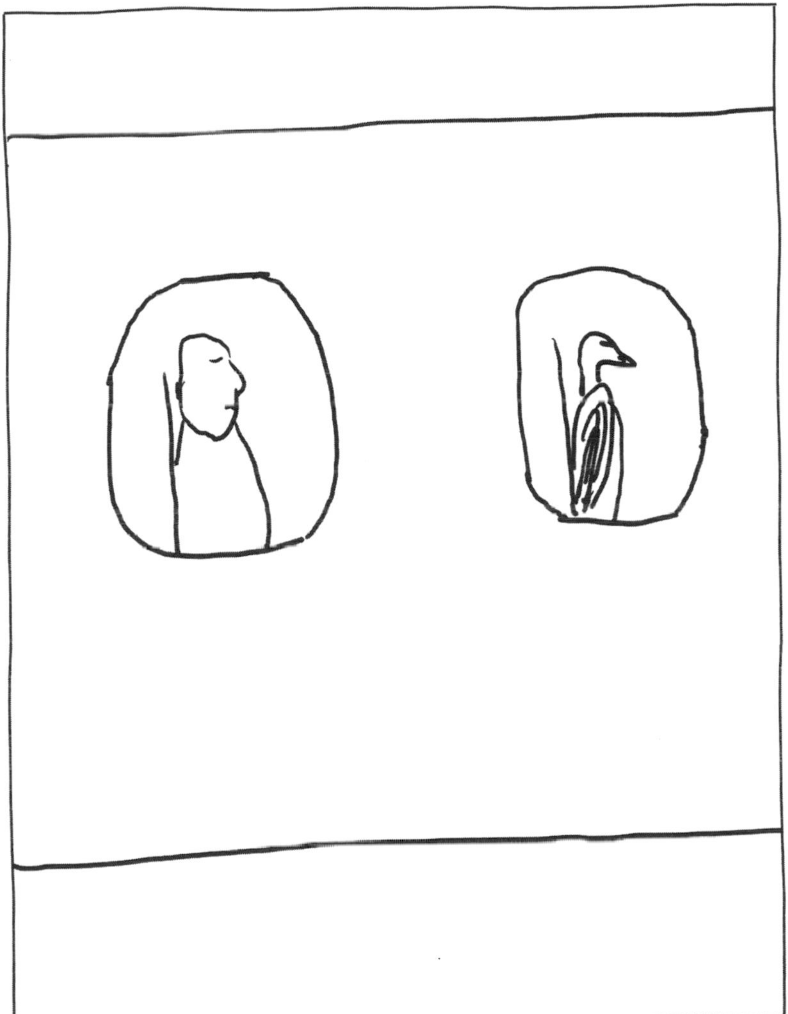

RICH BIRD FLYING SOUTH FOR THE WINTER

PIANO PLAYER'S TOOTHBRUSH

THE GREAT WALL OF CHINATOWN

Two necks. One heart.

ME LOOKING AT
THE PALM TREES
I BUILT.

Acknowledgments

Big thanks and lots of love to my mom, dad, and brother
for their tremendous support. I showed them many of
the drawings–often multiple versions–and their feedback
was very important. And they also did a lot of proof-
reading of the text.

The drawings in this book were done in various me-
diums: pen on paper, pencil on paper, as well as stylus
pen on both digital tablet and phone. Many were
drawn before I knew I was going to make a book–I
was just drawing for the sake of drawing. Many had
to be reformatted, and Kurt Iverson did the bulk of the
technical/computer work to get them ready for print.
I'd also like to thank my computer and scanner for not
breaking. And thank you, Lena Kim, for all your support and help.

Thanks to my book agent extraordinaire Richard
Abate for making things happen with Hachette Books.

Big thanks to my editor Paul Whitlatch not
only for his support and insight, but also for giving

me the artistic freedom to make the book I wanted to make. I also thank publisher Mauro DiPreta for green lighting this book. Art director Christopher Lin did a great job on the cover design. And I thank everyone else at Hachette who have all been a pleasure to work with: Michelle Aielli, executive director of publicity; Betsy Hulsebosch, director of marketing; Lauren Hummel, editorial assistant; Megan Gerrity, production editor; Odette Fleming, marketing assistant; and Emily Caldwell, publicity assistant.

Also thanks to Mike Weiss, Natalie Kim, Anja Jovic, Daisy Chen, Yvonne Mojica, Erin Bennett, Aparna Nancherla, Sara Benincasa, Ted Alexandro, Janeane Garofalo, Talia Kagan, Ryan Hamilton, and anyone to whom I showed a drawing to get feedback. And if there's anyone I mistakenly left out, I thank you as well.

And I thank you, who is holding this book right now, for having looked at my drawings.

ABOUT THE AUTHOR (definition)

The most pretentious section of a book.

It also reveals personal information, including the town where the author lives, which is quite useful to stalkers.

Now that you've finished
the book, let's see what
you have learned.

QUIZ

(correct answers on page 154)

1. In the book, what is your favorite character's social security number?

2. Who is the main protagonist in the book?

3. Which chapter solves racism?

4. On which page does the first plot point appear?

5. In two paragraphs, analyze the dénoument.

6. Which chapter was drawn in iambic pentameter?

7. What city is Scott from?

8. What is Scott's dog's favorite sandwich?

9. How many times does the letter E appear in the first three chapters?

10. Does Chapter 14 take place during late fall or early winter?

USE THESE PAGES TO MAKE YOUR OWN DRAWINGS.
AND SEND THEM TO ME. I'D LOVE TO SEE THEM.

IF YOU'RE STARTING HERE,

YOU'VE MADE A MAJOR MISTAKE.

THE BOOK ENDED PAGES AGO.